Christianity's Missing Peace

Christianity's Missing Peace

Pope Francis, Gospel Nonviolence, and the Renewal of the Irish Church

MARTIN McMULLAN

Foreword by Mairead Corrigan Maguire

WIPF & STOCK • Eugene, Oregon

CHRISTIANITY'S MISSING PEACE
Pope Francis, Gospel Nonviolence, and the Renewal of the Irish Church

Copyright © 2025 Martin McMullan. All rights reserved. Except for brief quotations in critical publications or reviews, no part of this book may be reproduced in any manner without prior written permission from the publisher. Write: Permissions, Wipf and Stock Publishers, 199 W. 8th Ave., Suite 3, Eugene, OR 97401.

Wipf & Stock
An Imprint of Wipf and Stock Publishers
199 W. 8th Ave., Suite 3
Eugene, OR 97401

www.wipfandstock.com

PAPERBACK ISBN: 979-8-3852-6195-6
HARDCOVER ISBN: 979-8-3852-6196-3
EBOOK ISBN: 979-8-3852-6197-0

VERSION NUMBER 11/21/25

Scripture quotations are from The Catholic Edition of the Revised Standard Version of the Bible, copyright © 1965, 1966 National Council of the Churches of Christ in the United States of America. Used by permission. All rights reserved worldwide

For my loving wife and beautiful children, my parents who embodied the principles of the gospel, and my unofficial mentors Father Emmanuel Charles McCarthy and Ciaron O'Reilly, and in loving memory of all who used the precious time of their lives to teach and live gospel nonviolence, in particular, Father Brian O'Toole and Peter McGuinness

To be true followers of Jesus today also includes embracing his teaching about nonviolence.... I pledge the assistance of the Church in every effort to build peace through active and creative nonviolence.

—Pope Francis, 2017 World Day of Peace message: "Nonviolence: A Style of Politics for Peace"

Contents

Foreword by Mairead Corrigan Maguire | ix
Preface | xi
Introduction | xv

1 Jesus and Nonviolence | 1
2 Early Christianity and Active Nonviolence | 31
3 Theologians and the Nonviolent Revolution of Jesus | 39
4 Towards a Papal Encyclical on Gospel Nonviolence? | 58
5 Gospel Nonviolence and the Renewal of the Irish Church | 74
6 A New Heaven and a New Earth | 104

Bibliography | 111

Foreword

JESUS' PLEA FROM THE cross, "Father, forgive them" (Luke 23:34), stands as the supreme act of nonviolent love, setting the clearest example for Christian discipleship. This moment embodies the radical ethic of *loving one's enemy* and *returning good for evil*, vividly illustrating that the commandment "do not kill" is not merely prohibitive but positively formative. It underscores the call to love even those who inflict suffering, offering mercy rather than retaliation.

The earliest Christians seem to have deeply absorbed this message. Biblical scholarship affirms that Jesus consistently rejected violence in all forms. As American Catholic biblical scholar John L. McKenzie famously remarked, "No reader of the New Testament... can retain any doubt of Jesus' position toward violence directed to persons... he rejected it totally."[1] This is not speculative theology but rigorous textual analysis: if Jesus did not completely reject violence, McKenzie concludes, then we can know nothing of him. Such a declaration compellingly challenges any moral framework, including the just war theory, as irreconcilable with the gospel's core.

St. Patrick, too, voiced this radical Christian commitment to non-killing. In his *Letter to the Soldiers of Coroticus*, Patrick condemns murder in no uncertain terms: "Do not kill. The murderer

---

1. McKenzie, *New Testament Without Illusion*, 248.

can have no part with Christ."[2] Within Christ, Patrick states, there is no space, even existentially, for killing. His appeal went beyond a doctrinal statement; it was a fervent moral plea motivated by love for those whose lives were endangered.

These historic voices—Jesus, McKenzie, Patrick—converge on a single point: Christian faith calls us to embrace nonviolence not as a concession, but as the essential path of love. Today, as global suffering mounts and the lives of millions of children are ravaged by war and deprivation, the church is in urgent need of a clear, courageous, and prophetic moral stance.

A papal encyclical explicitly rejecting the just war doctrine, affirming Christ's nonviolent way, and proclaiming Jesus' love and service as the means by which we save our world would provide such a stance. It would offer believers and nonbelievers alike witness to a love that refuses to respond to violence with violence, rooted not in political expedience, but in the sacrificial mercy of the Crucified One.

If the church does not speak with clarity now, in these dark days, then when? A renewed moral and spiritual vision, grounded in the nonviolent love of Christ, could rekindle hope across nations and generations.

This book has the potential to do precisely that: to embolden the faithful to *teach*, *live out*, and *embody* the radical love and service of Jesus, to help save our broken world.

Mairead Corrigan Maguire

---

2. Patrick, *Letter to the Soldiers*, §9.

Preface

ACCORDING TO CHRISTIAN FAITH, Jesus came into the world as the incarnation of God, not only to reveal the fullness of God's true nature but to offer salvation to humanity through his life, death, and resurrection. He invited his followers to share in this mission of salvation to heal a broken humanity from the wounds of evil and death. This involved imitating the God of love through a life of self-giving love modeled after his own, in which no violence was to be found. Somewhere along the line, however, the call to embody Christlike love, extending from friends to enemies, in every waking moment of a Christian's life, became obscured, and the matter of violence became a question of when it could be justified. For centuries, Christians have baptized empires, justified wars, and wielded power in Christ's name, but the Jesus of the Gospels never raised a sword and taught his followers to embody a way of nonviolence, even unto death.

The Catholic Church in Ireland, for its part, has long had to grapple with the question of justified violence throughout the history of the Irish nation. Ordinary Catholics will try in vain, however, to get any kind of uniform moral certainty from church authorities on the use of violence. The "just war" theory, first concocted by the pagan Roman philosopher Cicero, exists as a kind of loophole to enable Christians to join the ranks of armies throughout the world in good conscience. It is far from clear, though, when and how the principles of the "just war" can be applied and who gets to decide. It is this ambiguity that lies at the heart of a malaise, present within Christianity since the time of the Roman Emperor Constantine seventeen hundred years ago, that has led millions of Christians to take life and die on the battlefield, when it should never have been so. It has also seen Christians participate in grotesque acts of torture and public executions in a spirit of enmity and dehumanization on a systemic basis.

There is no such ambiguity coming from church authorities on other moral issues such as abortion, euthanasia, and homosexuality. The pro-life movement exists to protect the unborn child but for many of its supporters, the sacredness of life isn't a given ex utero. When it comes to the business of war and the taking of life, which is by far a much bigger problem in the world than engagement in culture wars, there has been a gross inconsistency to say the least. The nonviolent teachings and example of Jesus are shelved or explained away in a form that makes them irrelevant to daily living, and so it comes to pass that a Christian is able in good conscience to destroy another human being made in the image and likeness of God and remain in full communion with the church.

The Irish Church has a duty to teach its flock what Jesus has taught about love and nonviolence. To date, it has utterly failed to do so although it is not unique in this failure. This does not mean, however, that it cannot begin to change this egregious state of affairs. The Irish Church, like many of its sister churches throughout the world, is still well equipped to teach the truth of gospel nonviolence. Given the urgent crises that face humanity emanating from justified violence by human beings throughout the world towards one another and the environment, the time is ripe for Jesus' message of nonviolence to be heard and acted upon. As Irish politicians increase the country's military spending in line with the militarization policies of the EU, the prophetic voice of the Irish Church needs to be heard. Pope Francis has led the way on this, and the Irish Church needs to find courage to raise its voice for peace and nonviolence too. This can only be done, though, if a true understanding of gospel nonviolence and its revolutionary implications are grasped by church leaders and those who retain the Christian faith in Ireland. The implications for such a change of course are unknown and potentially frightening for a church that has suffered persecutions before. It may also seem futile to think that anything would change if Christians embodied Jesus' teachings on nonviolence in a world where might is still seen as right, but as the prayer of Oscar Romero eloquently puts it in relation to building the kingdom of God, "we are workers, not master builders."

This book is not intended to be a definitive discussion of Christian nonviolence and its opposition to justified violence. There are many books written by theologians and others that are excellent in explaining the centrality of nonviolence to the Christian revelation of God and that should be required reading for anyone seeking to deepen their Christian faith. Rather, I write as someone based in a country that is passing into a post-Catholic phase who still believes in Jesus and is still a member of the Catholic Church. My contention is that there are many believers in Ireland, and this is typically the case throughout the whole of the Christian church worldwide, that have never been taught or exposed to the most central and important truth of Christianity: Jesus reveals God to be a God of love who rejects violence in every circumstance and teaches his followers to imitate his example of nonviolence in the living out of God's will for humanity. The "Prince of Peace" who is born into the world and celebrated every Christmas is the only path to peace, and this path involves a total rejection of every kind of violence, no matter how justified it may seem. I write as someone born, reared, and living on the island of Ireland with its history of conflict and its complex relationship with a deeply embedded Christian tradition. This book, then, is an attempt to articulate, explain, and analyze the consequences of following Jesus in his path of nonviolent love of friends and enemies in a broadly Irish context. It deals mainly with the Catholic Church, and where the word "church" appears, it is usually referring to this.

The first chapters will give the scriptural basis for Jesus as the divine revelation of the nonviolent God and allude to some of the scholarly debate on this. The second chapter will discuss how gospel nonviolence was lived out by the first Christians despite much persecution, until the "Constantinian shift" in the fourth century and subsequent development of the just war theory distorted this radical praxis. The work of a selection of modern theologians will be explored, as will the contribution they each make to an understanding of the relevance and power of Jesus' nonviolent teachings and example for the present day. The following chapters will take a closer look at where the pronouncements of Pope Francis on Jesus' teachings of nonviolence have come from, which will involve an analysis of the statements of the various popes since Vatican II on the issues of war, peace, and social justice. Finally, I will explore the unique place and opportunities for the Irish Catholic Church to teach, preach, and live out active nonviolence as lived and taught by Jesus, and I will consider how a return of gospel nonviolence can be a truly transformative contribution to Christian unity and praxis in the world.

Introduction

IN THE WAKE OF the death of Pope Francis in April 2025, much has been written on what his legacy has been for the Catholic Church that he has led since his election in 2013. Pope Francis's papacy was controversial for some precisely because he emphasized and embodied parts of the gospel that for too long have been absent from the thoughts and practices of those at the leadership level of the Catholic Church. Through simple things like refusing to live in the Apostolic Palace, washing the feet of prisoners and Muslims, refusing to condemn homosexuals, and scolding bishops for displays of wealth, Pope Francis captured the hearts and minds of millions of Catholics and gained respect from many non-Catholics throughout the world for aligning his behaviors and words with those of the gospel. He divided opinion between conservative groups who abhorred what they considered breaking with church tradition and orthodoxy and those who believed he did not go far enough to modernize the church, particularly in terms of promoting women to priestly duties.

One aspect of his legacy, however, that deserves way more attention than it is likely to get is his unequivocal realignment of the church and the nonviolent Jesus. Gospel nonviolence is a topic that is inexplicably unfamiliar to most Christians throughout the world and yet so central to the manifestation of God in Jesus. Peace is a concept that is ever present in the thoughts and prayers of Christians worldwide, but more often than not, peace through the means

Introduction

of war is something that is tolerated. And, while maybe not liked, it leads to a justification of war-making and preparations for war for the contradictory purpose of peace. What Pope Francis has done, though, is to build on the previous work from various popes in the last decades to make active nonviolence as lived and taught by Jesus Christ central to how Christians are supposed to live their lives in faithful service to God's will and the building of the kingdom of God on earth as it is in heaven.

Many Christians have embodied and understood Jesus' teachings of nonviolence throughout the centuries, with the most recent famous examples being Martin Luther King Jr., Dorothy Day, Oscar Romero, Dan and Philip Berrigan, among many others. While these people in their own way have helped to build the consciousness of the kingdom of God as the nonviolent alternative to the violent structures that bind together the kingdoms of the world, they constitute only a small minority of Christians who have taken seriously Jesus' teaching to love at all costs. Gandhi, inspired as he was by the Sermon on the Mount as he took on the might of the British Empire and its war machine, once famously quipped that it was only Christians who failed to recognize Jesus as nonviolent. It begs the question as to what would happen if all or at least most Christians were imbued with the nonviolent Holy Spirit of God and tried to live in the nonviolent grace of God. As the biggest religion in the world, and with the Catholic Church in particular the biggest organization in the world, is it simplistic or naïve to hope or believe that the world could indeed be transformed by the nonviolent teachings of Jesus?

Peter Maurin (cofounder of the Catholic Worker) often remarked that the truth should be restated every twenty years. In a world where so much knowledge exists, often only with a few clicks of a mouse, there isn't necessarily the understanding that should go with this. In the digital age in which we are living, our minds are being rewired to very often scroll through articles and news without stopping for reflection to gain a critical understanding of what we have just encountered. "Fake news" is easily disseminated in this way. But what this book aims to uncover isn't an

Introduction

untruth so much as the wholesale ignorance of the most central part of Jesus' teaching and lived experience of the nature of God: God is nonviolent and calls Christians to a life of active nonviolence in imitation of his Son. This is not a new teaching on my behalf or a recent interpretation of the Gospels by some biblical scholar seeking to make a name for themselves. This is a truth that has been established ever since Christians have believed God entered human history in human form, and it has revolutionized world history as a result. It is a truth that the late Pope Francis recognized as a cornerstone of Christian practice in a world torn apart by conflict. It is also a truth that has the potential to renew in the most authentic way possible the Irish Catholic Church that has fallen so spectacularly from grace over the last number of decades.

This book serves as a humble attempt to articulate the truth of the nonviolent Jesus in a world that continues to suffer terribly by violence and division. It is not an exercise in mere intellectual meandering. Rather it is an urgent appeal to Christians to take seriously the nonviolence that Jesus the Son of God taught and lived right up to his death, resurrection, and ascension into heaven. Christians throughout the world at this moment in time are slaughtering each other and people of other faiths and nationalities in their thousands each year. If they are not directly involved in the slaughter they are encouraging and sending others to do the slaughter or making and investing in the weapons that will result in murder on an industrial scale. Still others by their silence in face of the slaughter are complicit in giving succor to those who oversee and benefit from the business of killing. The vast majority of these Christians will not give a moment's thought to what they are doing as being against their Christian faith because that is simply something they will have never heard anyone saying. Those with some bit of doubt will point to the just war theory to salve their consciences even though they may have a very rudimentary knowledge of what it is all about. Others will flag the Letter of St. Paul to the Romans where he tells his fellow Christians to submit to the authorities because they have been put in their positions of power by God himself. No conflict arises then when the government mandates its armies to kill the enemy in times of war because if it were wrong to do so then surely this would have been taught to them in their Christian schools. And so Christians in good conscience follow the orders of their governments and participate on a massive scale in the workings of the war machine throughout the world. This has been so for a long time in history and continues today, whether it is with regard to the war in Ukraine, the genocide in Palestine, or the slaughter in South Sudan, to mention but a few examples. The prayers of the faithful that call for peace at mass on any given Sunday typically ignore the reality of Christian participation in the dreadful business of war. Rather there is usually some hope expressed that God would give world leaders the courage to make peace instead of war in the world. The problem with such well-intentioned prayers, of course, is that they negate the individual responsibility of the ordinary Christian to refuse to cooperate in their government's war-making and do what they can to create the conditions for peace in the world inspired by the nonviolent teachings of Jesus.

This book is aimed first and foremost at the church faithful from a Catholic persuasion. Ireland, despite the scandals of the church, still retains its Christian heritage and remains a country deeply influenced by the Christian religion, even if today religion seems to have been banished from the public arena as something archaic but to be respected (so long as it is done in private and does not bother with participation in public affairs). The themes discussed in this book will nevertheless seem intolerable to a lot of people who retain their faith in the church and Christianity. Most Christians in Ireland and indeed the world are naturally nonviolent and abhor the use of violence. For many, though, this abhorrence will only extend to non-state perpetrators of violence. Many people are hostile to any suggestion that Christians are supposed to live totally nonviolent lives as Jesus taught and lived. It seems absurd in a world where resorting to violence is so often taken as normal and justified without a second's thought. Indeed, many Christians have relatives in the military (past or present) who have retained or indeed deepened their Christian faith, and to them the

Introduction

message of nonviolence is particularly distasteful. So, while as a church we celebrate the Prince of Peace at Christmastime and look forward to the peace on earth that his birth promises, it seems to be a step too far for some that the followers of Christ are supposed to become part of this journey towards peace. However, given the times of existential crisis that we are living in, I believe it an urgent task to awaken people to a central but forgotten and misunderstood tenet of Christianity that has the power to truly transform the world.

1

Jesus and Nonviolence

> Although each individual has a right to be respected in his own journey in search of the truth, there exists a prior moral obligation, and a grave one at that, to seek the truth and to adhere to it once it is known.
>
> —POPE JOHN PAUL II, *VERITATIS SPLENDOR*

IT CAN BE ARGUED that this search for truth that Pope Saint John Paul II wrote about is what makes us humans distinct among the rest of the creatures that inhabit this earth. In today's world, there is a popular notion that each person can have their own truth and live by it and that is fine. What is truth for one, might not be truth for another. Truth is therefore subjective. However, for Christians, Truth has a capital letter. Truth is not subject to the whims of the popular ideas of whatever particular age we happen to live in. Truth is independent of whether we as people accept it to be true or not. Truth is not relative. Instead it is wrapped up in the mystery of God. That we can never fully grasp this mystery is both equally frustrating and very humbling. To the person who has grown skeptical about Christian faith, it is an exercise in make-believe.

However, it is a Christian duty to search for the discernible truth about God insofar as it can be grasped through reason and faith and to live this truth faithfully in daily life.

The ultimate source of truth for the Christian is God, and we find out about God through our study and experience of his incarnate Son's life and teachings in the Gospels and the broader New Testament. Jesus proclaimed that he and the Father are one and therefore he is "the way, and the truth, and the life" (John 14:6). Once Christians have discovered the truth from this ultimate source, everything else that is presented to us in our lives must be viewed through this prism. This immediately puts the Christian at odds with what passes for common wisdom and accepted societal norms. This can be seen none more so than when it comes to the issue of violence and what makes for peace in our world.

The commandment of Jesus to love as he loves is the new commandment that he taught to his closest followers before his torture and execution at the hands of the powers that be, who couldn't tolerate such teaching gaining sway among people lest it disrupted their privileged positions as religious leaders and political elites. This commandment lies at the heart of the Christian revolution and inaugurates the kingdom of God as a reality on earth. Christians are called by God to share in the living reality of this kingdom by their words and deeds, with the teachings and example of Jesus along with the Holy Spirit as their guide. The centerpiece of this new dawn in human history is God's absolute rejection of the use of violence by the people he loved into existence. Jesus teaches and lives a life of perfect nonviolence all the way to enduring a horrible death at the hands of evil men. His resurrection from the dead is the triumph of love over evil and death, the most marvelous intervention of God ever in human history and one that leads to the salvation of all who choose to believe it. It leads to salvation because it emphatically proves for the believer that the power of love is stronger than the power of evil and death. A life spent trying to live in the spirit of Christian love is a life that bears witness to the faith that Christlike love is eternal and all powerful (attributes of God) and leads to the salvation not only of all souls, but also of the world. The Christian, then, chooses love as the highest moral guide even when this will lead to martyrdom and mortal death.

This is at once terribly frightening and ultimately reassuring for the Christian believer. The revelation of Jesus that God is love, the father of all and rich in mercy, who expects from those he loved into existence merciful love towards one another in order to share in the likeness of God, seems fairly straightforward to the Christian believer who grows up in the faith; but in reality, it is a dreadfully difficult and scary leap into the unknown. Doubts about whether there is an afterlife and whether God is real are perfectly natural thoughts for the Christian to ponder, but once these have been overcome, a fully engaged Christian faith emerges that is transformative not just for the individual believer but for the community and world in which they reside.

The Gospels and the New Testament of course are the point of reference for the Christian believer, and in them they will see how the person of Jesus inspired and frightened in equal measure—and how his closest companions had to experience all the drama of the crucifixion and resurrection to finally understand the words of their master. Their response to these events ultimately gave us the Christian church that has grown like a mustard seed to become the biggest of all the religions in the world. Perhaps that may explain the complacency among some Christians that the work is pretty much done, and we simply need to have what we hold. However, the kingdom of God remains a reality unfulfilled, and the missionary work of the Christian therefore is as urgent today as it was two thousand years ago. This missionary work, however, cannot be allowed to take on the character of a lot of previous methodologies for spreading the faith. It will be forever a dreadful stain on the Christian conscience the days when the "faith" was spread with so-called Christians bearing a sword in one hand and a Bible in the other. Nor is the Christian faith to be spread through fear or salvation something to be bought. Worst of all is the practice of using the Christian religion as a means to control whole populations— the "opium of the people" as Marx called it[1]—so that the people

---

1. Marx, *Contribution*, 49.

will know their place and, though their lives may be miserable in this world, will concentrate on looking forward to the next. Rather, missionary work has to be carried out in the spirit of Jesus, who promised people the fullness of life. His teachings and example are the means to break the systems of domination in the world and create conditions where human beings live in dignity and can flourish as God intended. His message of liberation will not be accepted by everyone, but that is where the church must have the courage to break with the powers that be and live faithfully until such times that the whole earth is redeemed and heaven and earth become full of the glory of the nonviolent God who is love. That is the Christian hope and as such the mission that they are to embark on in their individual and collective lives. To this end, knowledge and understanding of the unique and revolutionary teachings of the nonviolent Jesus are indispensable.

A great deal of biblical scholarship and theological debate has centered on the nonviolent teachings of Jesus to his disciples and whether they could possibly form the basis of intended ethical behavior for his followers. A plethora of hermeneutic issues arise when applying the Bible to politics and formulating principles for reading the Bible politically. Chief among these for considering whether Jesus reveals God as nonviolent and establishes an ethic of active nonviolence as a central practice for Christians wishing to live in the kingdom of God he inaugurated are: the relation between the Old and New Testaments and the problem of the selective use of texts to justify contemporary positions; the question of whether ethical principles that appear in Scripture relate to personal or public morality; applying the proper literary and historical context to biblical passages that aid our understanding about what they mean and if they speak to us today in our modern setting; and the dangers inherent in manipulating texts to support preconceived attitudes and projects.[2] Despite the widely diverse viewpoints that interpretation of the Scriptures brings up, since the mid-twentieth century there have been numerous seminal works illuminating the nonviolence of Jesus, leaving little scholarly

---

2. Bauckham, *Bible in Politics*, 3–19.

doubt that the message of nonviolence was a central part of Jesus' teaching and life practice and informed the faith lives of those in the early Christian church.[3] The following section offers a brief overview of some of the scriptural exegesis on gospel nonviolence, concentrating on the Sermon on the Mount and Jesus' ministry in the context of first-century Palestine.

VIOLENCE IN FIRST-CENTURY PALESTINE AND JESUS' NONVIOLENT ALTERNATIVE

Renowned twentieth-century biblical scholar John L. McKenzie, SJ, asserted in one of his excellent books that "if Jesus did not reject any type of violence for any purpose, then we know nothing of him."[4] This is despite the fact that violence was a constant feature of everyday life in the world of first-century Palestine into which Jesus was born, with the harshness of a violent Roman occupation taking its toll on the ordinary people. Jesus grew up in the region of Galilee and would no doubt have been aware of the contemporary violent events sparked by the murderous rage of the people against their oppressors. The issue of taxes and having to pay for the upkeep of Roman armies and their wars, and for the lavish building programs of King Herod and his dynasty, contributed to a violent revolt led by Judas the Galilean around 4 BCE. This was put down by the Roman general Varus who sent his army into the countryside and crucified around two thousand suspects.[5] Such rebellions and customary brutal methods at crushing the attempts of the people to free themselves from foreign occupation were nothing new in a land that had known violence and conquest for most of the history of the Hebrew nation. The message of peace that Jesus taught and embodied by his actions was therefore not preached in a vacuum but in the context of social and political turmoil. It was aimed at real solutions to concrete problems and

---

3. Rynne, "Jesus and Nonviolence," 80.
4. McKenzie, *New Testament Without Illusion*, 252.
5. Rynne, "Jesus and Nonviolence," 83.

designed not only to save the individual soul but the whole world, crucially offering an alternative to the traditional responses that were on offer.[6]

Those traditional responses were typified by different groups in Palestine at that time and consisted of flight, accommodation, or fight. The Essenes fled to the desert, according to the Dead Sea Scrolls, and attempted to construct their own version of the Jewish religion away from the contamination of worldly problems. The priests and the Herodians opted for accommodation with the Romans and so could practice their religion so long as this did not interfere with Roman authority, and as a consequence, they could accumulate a degree of power and wealth for themselves. The Pharisees, who were later to become the party of violent resistance during the Jewish revolt in 65 CE, embodied the "Zealot" option, which came to be a term used for those who saw armed rebellion as the only effective means to end Roman oppression in their land. They maintained their religious purity by not associating with pagans and were to the fore in promoting nationalist sentiment in Jesus' time.[7]

The alternative way that Jesus presented to Israel, and ultimately to the world, was the building up of an inclusive community based on the principle of nonviolent *agapē* love, daring to risk even the love of enemies and being open to the prospect of suffering to achieve the goal of this renewed society. The New Testament can be seen as the cumulative record of this pronouncement by Jesus that God is the God of peace and love itself (1 John 4: 7–21). The kingdom of God that Jesus proclaimed was not *of* this world, according to John's Gospel (John 18:36), because it involved a rejection of the dominative logic that ran through the destructive structures of the kingdoms of the world that brought slavery and misery to the many. However, there were very real social, economic, and political implications to Jesus' proclamation of the kingdom that were to define his mission. In light of this, Jesus can be characterized

---

6. Musto, *Catholic Peace Tradition*, 20.
7. Rynne, "Jesus and Nonviolence," 84.

as fulfilling the Old Testament prophesies of the Son of Man, the suffering servant, and Emmanuel, the Prince of Peace.[8]

Trying to find an overall synthesis of the Bible has occupied the lifetimes of many biblical scholars, but despite their efforts, debates and disagreements persist. Jesus as the culmination of the Old Testament story and at the same time the revelation of God as a God of nonviolence is seen as problematic by many biblical scholars who question the exegesis at play. One proposed solution for explaining how God can be portrayed as ordering massacres in one breath in the Old Testament and then suddenly being an opponent of any violence in the New Testament was put forward by J. Denny Weaver. He suggested that because the Old Testament was a historical record of how God's people came to develop their understanding of God and how their God worked in the world, it was natural that different views of God would appear. Weaver was of the view that attempting to harmonize and synthesize all biblical statements on any particular question was the wrong approach, and so it became necessary to say that some ideas in Scripture are wrong, misguided, or can be abandoned.[9] For the multitude of accounts and images of God supporting violence to punish evil or exact vengeance in the Old Testament, there are many occurrences where God supports nonviolent solutions, especially from the time of Jeremiah onwards. A conflicted view of the character of God becomes apparent in the Old Testament but, in Jesus, the nonviolent trajectory of the Old Testament is carried forward to its fullest expression, with the resurrection confirming the character of God as the God of life over the powers of the world characterized by the darkness of violent domination.[10] Following this logic, it is in the Gospels that God is fully revealed as nonviolent with the incarnation of Jesus, who embodies a counterculture to imperial domination.

From the very beginning of the Gospel of Mark, the logic of violence at the heart of the Roman world is challenged. Mark 1:1, "The beginning of the Gospel of Jesus Christ, the Son of God," in

---

8. Musto, *Catholic Peace Tradition*, 21.
9. Weaver, *Nonviolent God*, 90–95.
10. Weaver, *Nonviolent God*, 104–18.

which the narrator says nothing controversial to the casual observer today, is in fact subversively resisting the predominant political values of the empire and calling people to recognize in Jesus the heralding of a new kind of kingdom that breaks ranks completely from the old world of violence, misery, and injustice. Mark uses the word "gospel" deliberately, as to his readers it was understood as "news of victory," particularly in military battles. In his usage, there is no military victory for Jesus; there is a nonviolent death instead, a seeming violent defeat. Roman propaganda would also have eulogized Caesar as the "divine man," and so Mark subverts the claim of the Roman emperor to divinity by instead proclaiming divinity to belong to the one whom the empire had brutally executed but who, through his resurrection, had manifested fully the glory of God over the powers of evil and death.[11] Mark recognizes in Jesus from the very outset that the nonviolent realm of God will necessarily lead to a clash with the imperial culture and its legitimating myths but that faith in this divine project will ultimately result in triumph.

The Magnificat found in the Gospel of Luke serves as the nonviolent manifesto of Jesus. Though the Magnificat is spoken by Mary, the mother of Jesus, it foreshadows the values and mission of Jesus himself, and can indeed be read as a radical, prophetic declaration of a new social order grounded in justice, mercy, and nonviolence. There is no call to arms or vengeance, but rather it expresses God's intention to raise up the humble and oppressed in a reversal of worldly power: "He has brought down the mighty from their thrones, and exalted those of humble estate; he has filled the hungry with good things, and the rich he has sent away empty" (Luke 1:52–53). This song of praise is a subversive act as it glorifies God and defiles all the other would-be gods of Caesar, wealth, and domination by declaring allegiance to the Lord of love. The Magnificat prefigures much of Jesus' teaching and serves as the spiritual and ethical foundation for his entire ministry.

The temptation stories found in their fullest expression in the Gospels of Luke and Matthew offer further clarification that Jesus' mission was to proclaim the kingdom of God as a new departure

---

11. Myers, *Binding the Strong Man*, 123–24.

from the modus operandi of how the other worldly kingdoms functioned. Wealth, status, and worldly power are rejected as means by which Jesus is to carry out the will of God. They are in total contrast to the values of the kingdom of God where equality, humility, and servanthood abound. The reign of Satan has come to an end with the breaking into history of God's new kingdom of peace and nonviolence.

THE TEACHINGS OF NONVIOLENCE AT THE CENTER OF THE SERMON ON THE MOUNT

The Sermon on the Mount as detailed in the Gospels of Matthew and Luke is the epicenter of the teachings on nonviolence by Jesus. Within this sermon, Jesus not only challenges prevailing attitudes towards retaliation and enemy hatred but also offers a radically alternative vision rooted in love, mercy, and peacemaking. Jesus is seen to be openly contradicting the law of the Old Testament in Matt 5:38–39: "You have heard that it was said, 'An eye for an eye, and a tooth for a tooth.' But I say to you, Do not [violently] resist one who is evil.'" Far from promoting passivity in the face of violence and injustice, contemporary exegesis has found that Jesus promotes the opposite: creative nonviolent resistance.[12]

Three examples of creative nonviolent responses to situations of violent injustice are relayed by Jesus to his listeners. In the first instance, the instruction to turn the other cheek was not advice of what to do in fisticuffs, but rather about standing up to an abusive superior who would be prone to strike people they felt beneath them in status with the back of their hand, and thus on the right cheek as indicated in Matthew's Gospel. The person who had received the blow would be challenging the abuser to punch them in the face at the cost of lowering themselves to an equal status, and in doing so would refuse both to cower in a humiliated fashion and to respond in kind with violence.

---

12. Lohfink, *Jesus and Community*, 53.

In the second instance, if a person is dragged into court as a result of an unpaid debt and Deut 24:10–13 is enacted, where a creditor can take the cloak as collateral, a person who also gives over the undergarment to the creditor will be making a statement that a judicial system that leaves people in such dire straits as to be naked as the day they were born is unfair. For the followers of Jesus, debt and securing daily bread were at the forefront of the preoccupations of daily life for a peasant, as reflected in the Lord's Prayer. Debt and exorbitant interest were a real source of anger for people, and by stripping naked in a court dealing with this issue, Jesus' followers would have exposed, in a creatively nonviolent manner, the cruelty of these structures and the pretense of justice that went with them.

The third example refers to the Roman occupation of the country and the Roman soldiers' right, according to their code, to press into service a member of the occupied land to carry his pack weighing thirty to forty kilograms for one mile. The restriction on one mile was to limit the resentment of the local population, and a soldier caught abusing that privilege could warrant punishment from his centurion. Therefore, taking the initiative to walk the second mile was the person refusing to be looked on as someone without power by taking an action that could easily land the Roman soldier into trouble.[13]

In these examples Jesus can be seen counseling his followers to act against domination by using their imagination, courage, and strength. He gave them a new ethic to live by that went beyond the golden rule of loving one's neighbor as oneself. This new ethic was the love of enemies in imitation of God, who "makes his sun rise on the evil and on the good, and sends rain on the just and on the unjust" (Matt 5:45). This was a stark and explicit rejection of both Jewish and pagan ethics and was to distinguish the members of the new kingdom from the old. In Matt 5:48, Jesus taught these prospective citizens of the new order, "You therefore must be perfect, as your heavenly Father is perfect." And to do so would require a

---

13. Wink, *Powers That Be*, 104.

complete change of heart, a *metanoia* to the ways of love that bring such a nonviolent kingdom of peace and justice into being.[14]

SCHOLARLY DEBATES ON THE INTERPRETATION OF THE SERMON ON THE MOUNT

Given the lofty nature of the ethical standards demanded by Christ in the Sermon, however, the history of its interpretation has been dominated by attempts by some biblical scholars to downplay its significance or to moderate its radical demands in all kinds of creative ways.[15] For other biblical scholars, these passages convey the essence of Christian peacemaking, describing how nonviolence lies at the heart of it. It is a radical break from the past as Jesus reveals God as a God of nonviolent love of friends and enemies.[16]

Richard Horsley was one of the leading biblical scholars to oppose any basis for reading a doctrine of nonviolence into the text of the Sermon on the Mount. He rejected the idea that the ethical exhortations of Christ amounted to absolute rules or universalized models of conduct.[17] A key point for Horsley hinged on the interpretation of who constituted the "enemies" of Jesus' listeners at that time. He maintained that Jesus was not referring to foreign, national, or domestic political enemies of Israel but rather to local adversaries who might negatively affect the interpersonal relations that his followers experienced on a daily basis. Therefore the sayings related to loving one's enemies and being merciful were broad commands or exhortations regarding social relations focused on praxis for the coming kingdom of God, unrelated to violent situations.[18] Consequently, then, Horsley was able to assert that Jesus was not rejecting the Zealot option of violence in the collection of sayings in the Sermon on the Mount in favor of nonviolence, as

14. Musto, *Catholic Peace Tradition*, 24–25.
15. Searle, "Is the Sermon," 38.
16. Musto, *Catholic Peace Tradition*, 21.
17. Horsley, "Ethics and Exegesis," 4.
18. Musto, *Catholic Peace Tradition*, 21.

the issue of political violence for liberation from oppression simply wasn't the issue in these texts. He believed the Zealots to be "a modern scholarly myth" and certainly not something that was in the mind of the Gospel writers.[19]

Horsley was disputed in his assertions by New Testament theologian Richard Hays, however, who claimed that Horsley's interpretation of "enemies" in Matt 5:44 was erroneous. For Hays, the Greek word, *echthroi*, was a generic term and often used in biblical Greek to refer to national or military enemies, not just to personal or local ones. Furthermore, Hays claimed that there was nothing in the Matthean context to suggest any precise social situation entailing village squabbles or conflicts that Horsley felt Jesus was addressing.[20]

In addition, biblical theologian Walter Wink, in his "translation" of New Testament semantics, which he believed had become too spiritualized in a modern setting, paved a way for theologically grounding nonviolence as a way of life promoted by Jesus in the sociopolitical context of the Bible and its resistance to empire. He viewed the interpretation of "Do not resist one who is evil" (Matt 5:39) to refer directly to an exhortation to nonviolence. The verb "resist" in this translation of the Greek in Matthew, *antistēnai*, was translated by Wink to refer to "a potentially lethal disturbance or armed rebellion," and so in effect the verse in question should have read, "Don't react violently to evil."[21] For Wink, however, any kind of pacifism espoused by Christians as being passive in the face of evil wasn't being faithful to the teachings of Jesus on active nonviolence. Jesus' third way of responding to evil, as referenced in the Sermon on the Mount, wasn't passive or violent; it was calling Christians to resist evil in a nonviolent way that forces the oppressor to make choices they would rather not make.

A powerful exegesis on the Sermon on the Mount by biblical theologian Glen Stassen offered a way past some of the attempts to downplay its radical ethical demands. He was responding to

---

19. Horsley, "Ethics and Exegesis," 13–14.
20. Hays, *Moral Vision*, 328.
21. Wink, *Engaging the Powers*, 227.

renowned twentieth-century ethicist Reinhold Niebuhr, who had revived the school of thought regarding the counsel to perfection in Matt 5:48, saying that it was an impossible ideal but one that Christians should strive towards as it represented the highest end of human moral endeavor and would contribute positively to the "ordinary" morality of humankind.[22] Stassen labeled such interpretations as belonging to a "hermeneutics of evasion" that allowed Christians to ignore Jesus' teachings and instead find some other source for following a more "pragmatic ethic."[23]

For Stassen the teachings of Jesus from the Sermon on the Mount were a realistic ethic for discipleship and could guide human conduct in the present-day setting. He argued that the Sermon consisted of "fourteen triads," each one containing a teaching on (1) traditional righteousness, (2) a vicious cycle, and (3) a transforming initiative. In the first instance Jesus was calling his disciples' attention to traditional righteousness that they "have heard," usually from the Torah or elsewhere in the Hebrew Scriptures, for example in the commandment against murder (Matt 5:21). Jesus then went on to diagnose the vicious cycle surrounding the action of the sin that led to the prohibition in traditional teaching. In the case of murder, it was anger that led to the sin and that, left unchecked, could result in a vicious cycle leading to reciprocal murder taking place, given the simple fact of the human condition. It is in the third triad, the "transforming initiative," that Jesus' life-giving teaching is made accessible to his disciples. In the case of anger, imperatives were used for the first time in the triad: "So if you are offering your gift at the altar, and there remember that your brother has something against you, leave your gift there before the altar and go; first be reconciled to your brother, and then come and offer your gift" (Matt 5:23-24). Far from giving a command to embody an impossible ideal, he instructed his followers to take initiatives that would free them from the vicious cycles of anger, resentment, counter-judgment, and potential violence.[24]

22. Niebuhr, *Interpretation of Christian Ethics*, 124.
23. Stassen, *Just Peacemaking*, 33.
24. Stassen, "Fourteen Triads," 267-308.

These "transforming initiatives" were the fulfillment of the Torah and offered a way of deliverance based on God's grace. By participating in these active nonviolent initiatives of discipleship, Christians were participating in God's salvation.[25]

JESUS' ACTIVE NONVIOLENCE IN HIS MISSION

In the life events of Jesus recorded in the Gospels that constituted his mission, Jesus followed his own teachings of active and creative nonviolence time and again when faced with the violently oppressive structures of a society that kept people downtrodden and with opponents who wanted to kill him. He saved a woman caught in adultery from the consequences of an oppressive law against women that demanded the death penalty by stoning but let the man off the hook. He courageously walked into the middle of this crowd and put them back on their heels by uttering a devastating critique of their behavior in the famous one-liner, "Let him who is without sin among you be the first to throw a stone" (John 8:7). He further challenged the structures of Jewish society that dehumanized the sick and the destitute by healing lepers, thus restoring them to live again in community, and he attacked the temple institution for robbing money from widows, who were among the poorest in Jewish society: "It is written, 'My house shall be a house of prayer'; you have made it a den of robbers" (Luke 19:46). He healed on the Sabbath and in doing so brought the wrath of the Pharisees upon himself, obsessed as they were with maintaining religious purity even when it meant further burdening the already overburdened people with more laws and obligations.

Jesus' inclusive community building and peacemaking were more than simply winning over individual hearts and minds to internal change. Israel at the time of Jesus was a religious, cultural, and political entity that, despite living under the domination of various foreign powers, retained its hope that political freedom and peace would be brought by the Messiah, in fulfillment of God's

---

25. Schlabach, "'Confessional' Nonviolence," 133.

promise. Inasmuch as Jesus conceived of himself as the Messiah, he fully shared this aspiration for liberation. However, he rejected completely the use of physical force to fulfill his messianic role and the narrow nationalistic expectations that went with it.[26] The new kingdom that he proclaimed was to be wholly different in structure than the known kingdoms of the world. His disciples were instructed not to lord it over one another but rather become the servants of all. There was to be a redistribution of wealth so that everyone in the community would be able to enjoy the abundance of God's bounty on a daily basis. Forgiveness and mercy were to be the defining features of Christian communities, where the poor and marginalized were to be included. In its very essence the new kingdom of God was to be nonviolent in structure and as a result would inevitably clash with the violent structures of the empire. Jesus foretold persecution for his followers but did not give them any recourse for violent defense of the kingdom.

The consequences of this choice to reject the temptation of violent means in favor of active nonviolence were immediate and led to Jesus being abandoned first by the large following he had amassed during his nonviolent campaign in the countryside, but also by his closest associates who had never fully understood or accepted the "way of the cross" as the difficult path in following Jesus. His refusal to inflict suffering would inevitably lead to his passion and humiliating death on the cross. In the Garden of Gethsemane Jesus rejected the use of armed self-defense and ordered the disciple who cut off the ear of the servant of the high priest, "Put your sword back into its place; for all who take the sword will perish by the sword" (Matt 26:52). If ever violence was to be justified or divinely sanctioned in all of human history it was in defense of the one they believed was the holy Son of God, and yet Jesus lived by his own teachings, choosing instead to love his enemies even when faced with the prospect of a horribly violent death.[27] In his last act before his freedom was seized by men of violence, Jesus chose to heal the ear of the servant in an act of

---

26. Musto, *Catholic Peace Tradition*, 25.
27. Crossan, *God and Empire*, 178.

selfless love for his enemies. Finally, while hanging in excruciating agony on the cross Jesus embodied perfect nonviolence by praying for his executioners in a manner consistent with his message about the centrality of forgiveness in the kingdom: "Father, forgive them; for they know not what they do" (Luke 23:34).[28]

In confronting the powers of his time Jesus was bearing witness to the truth of his own teaching and his faithfulness to God's will that resulted in the defeat of the powers with the triumph of the resurrection.[29] The New Testament records the growth in faith of the first Christians as they grappled with this new reality and new understanding of Jesus as Lord. Paul, in his Letter to the Romans, written before the Gospels, encapsulated the spirit of the Gospels and the primitive church by exhorting his readers to practice the principles of peacemaking that resonated in the Sermon on the Mount, saying, "Overcome evil with good" (Rom 12:21). These remarks on nonviolence serve as an introduction on Paul's well-known appeal to submit to the higher authorities (Rom 13:1–7). Far from being an instruction on acquiescence to political power, Paul was laying out for the Christian the teaching of Jesus to overcome evil with love. One does not violently resist domination that is evil with physical weapons but rather uses moral and spiritual means to ultimately defeat and transform the human kingdoms of the world in imitation of Christ. The means and the ends are consistent, and though this method of nonviolent peacemaking may lead to suffering, it is suffering that is redemptive and renews the face of the earth.

THE ATONEMENT CONTROVERSY

Other passages from Paul, however, are highlighted by critics of the idea of a nonviolent God, especially in respect to those that lean towards a "satisfaction" theory of atonement. There are a lot of sacrificial references, not only in Hebrews, but in the sacrificial

---

28. Rynne, "Jesus and Nonviolence," 91.
29. Wink, *Engaging the Powers*, 227.

hermeneutic used by Paul himself in his other texts, which depict the violent death of Jesus as something God required in order to atone for the sins of the people. Romans 3:25, where Christ is appointed as a sacrifice for atonement by the shedding of his blood, and Gal 3:10–14 are among the clearest expressions of the substitutionary nature of Jesus' atonement in the New Testament in appeasing the wrath of God. The notion that the death of a willing and innocent victim could make atonement with the gods or God for the sins of the people was a popular idea at that time among Greeks, Jews, and Romans and may explain Paul's understanding of Christ's death.[30] Likewise, the idea of the death of Christ as a sacrificial atonement is to be found in other significant areas of the New Testament. For example, in both Mark 10:41, where Jesus is said to give his life as a ransom for many, and 1 Pet 2:22–25, there are allusions to the suffering servant who dies sacrificially for the sins of the people. Here it is argued that Christ bore the sins that led to his death as an innocent substitute for God's sinful people.[31] Depending on which view of the atonement Christians take from Scripture, contested views of God are at stake: a God of loving mercy and radical nonviolence or a vengeful God who demands justice even when it involves the bloody murder of his own Son.

RENÉ GIRARD AND ATONEMENT

Here, it is useful to introduce the work of French anthropologist René Girard, a committed Catholic, whose insights on the Bible and human sacrifice have greatly aided the understanding of Jesus' death and resurrection as the foundation stone for the radical nonviolent kingdom of God breaking into history. His work deserves to be communicated to a wider audience than the select group of theologians who understand the groundbreaking insights he discovered on human nature and its relevance to the Bible and Christianity.

---

30. Thielman, "Atonement," 109–11.
31. Thielman, "Atonement," 115.

In offering a critical evaluation on René Girard's use of biblical texts in formulating a doctrine of atonement, it is important to state that he never purposefully set out to formulate a comprehensive theory of atonement in the way a theologian might do. Rather, his was "a search for the anthropology of the Cross, which turns out to rehabilitate orthodox theology."[32] Girard's work in trying to aid theologians has caused immense controversy as well as inspiring lots of admirers who have taken on the task of evaluating how his work helps further a Christian understanding of the cross of Jesus that stands at the center of Christian faith.

AN ANTHROPOLOGICAL UNDERSTANDING ON THE ORIGINS OF VIOLENT SOCIETIES

Girard's controversial theory on human nature and human culture stems from an analysis of human desires that he calls "mimetic" desire, which can lead to violence as competing rivals battle each other over desirable objects. This violence would have been unceasing in early human cultures and would ultimately have led to their decimation had they not found a mechanism for containing the conflict. And this, Girard expounds, was found in the human propensity for "scapegoating." This happened at some stage in the cycle of mimetic violence when the community turned on one of its members as the cause for all the chaos. The destruction of such a scapegoat produced such a genuinely unifying experience that over time the hated scapegoat was turned into a god, such was the peace and relief it brought to the society. The effect of this original lynching would then be commemorated ritually and sacrificially in an attempt to perpetuate its peace-bringing effect, and so ritualized violence became the basis for religion, mythology, monarchy, and the establishment of hierarchical status-based societies in order to bring about internal peace.[33]

---

32. Williams, *Girard Reader*, 287.
33. McDonald, "Violence and the Lamb Slain," 346–47.

THE TRANSFORMATIVE POWER OF THE GOSPELS IN BREAKING THE CYCLE OF EVIL

Girard brings this anthropological analysis to the Bible and finds throughout the Old Testament, from the very beginning, a divinely inspired working out of the scapegoat mechanism, found explicitly in Lev 16 but not used much in Girard's work. A complete understanding is never quite fully developed until the Christ event. He sees the Gospels relate the most important event in history in which this whole process, which characterizes the realm of Satan, is revealed and exposed by the crucifixion of Jesus, who is the innocent victim slain by the "powers and principalities" who were unaware that they were participating in their own ultimate downfall.[34] In contrast to myths that carry similar narratives to the Gospels, the story of Jesus is told from the viewpoint that he is an innocent victim and that the "powers and principalities" have connived wrongly against him. The crucifixion happens as a consequence of sinful humanity and the human relations that give effect to mimetic contagion, which is the same thing as Satan, according to Girard.[35] What results from this is revolutionary in the respect that the power of Satan over humanity has been broken by the revealing of the scapegoat mechanism and the false peace that it brings to the world through violence. The Holy Spirit–guided alternative community of the kingdom of God—started by the small number of Jesus' faithful disciples after the resurrection, constituting values of forgiveness, peace, mercy, and nonviolence—breaks out onto history and will be fully established eschatologically at the fullness of time.[36]

---

34. Girard, *I See Satan Fall*, 138.
35. Girard, *I See Satan Fall*, 142.
36. Girard, *I See Satan Fall*, 188–89.

GIRARD AND THE *CHRISTUS VICTOR* VIEW ON ATONEMENT

Girard's work ties in eminently with the *Christus Victor* view of atonement, which became the dominant idea of the atonement during the time of the early church.[37] This view maintained that Christ overcame the powers and principalities that held humanity in bondage by his death on the cross and his victorious resurrection. This breaking of enslavement to the "powers and principalities" led to the reconciliation between God and humanity and the defeat of Satan. For Girard then, the death of Christ cannot be viewed in sacrificial terms, and therefore the predominant view of the church since Anselm, known as the satisfaction theory, is invalid because it continues to buy into the very scapegoating mechanism that the Gospels seek to expose and subvert.[38] It is precisely here that Girard's use and rejection of biblical texts has come into question and led to some fairly heated commentaries given the weight of the issue at stake.

THE CHALLENGE OF GIRARD TO BIBLICAL SCHOLARSHIP

The main cause of surprise and a certain amount of scandal among biblical scholars and theologians was Girard's way of brashly laying his claims across such a widespread range of disciplines as anthropology, psychology, literary criticism, biblical studies, and theology.[39] Girard's new hermeneutic for understanding the Bible with its culmination in the Christ event was a theory of religion that seriously challenged many previously held beliefs and made some sweeping claims about them in the process. Burton Mack, writing in 1985, by which time Girard's works had been translated and were causing a stir among a wider audience, claimed that Girard had achieved "nothing less than an invasion of the field

---

37. Aulen, *Christus Victor*, 22.
38. Girard, *Things Hidden*, 175.
39. Kirwan, *Discovering Girard*, 62.

of biblical scholarship," whereby traditional scholarship would see his use of biblical texts as idiosyncratic.[40] He was accused of ignoring the biblical scholars' "historical-literary criticism" approach to the Bible, which was bound to be upsetting for them.[41] Other scholars had issues with Girard applying anthropology to the biblical texts and trying to force results to make the text fit into his grand theory, almost casually generalizing large swathes of Old Testament texts to fit his purpose.[42] Michael Kirwan has attempted to defend Girard's use of the biblical texts by locating his method in figural interpretation, whereby the figure of Christ, through his cross and resurrection, is understood as the hermeneutical key for interpreting Old Testament passages that refer to figures like Adam, Moses, or Abraham or to specific events like the crossing of the Red Sea.[43] Criticisms of Girard's work either as a whole or in certain details, though, usually ended up with a recognition that it was full of new insights to the biblical revelation and challenged religious thought in a profound way.[44]

By way of illustrating some of the controversies surrounding Girard's use of biblical texts, I will critically evaluate some that illuminate an explanation of the atonement: first, his critique of the story of Job, then the account of the servant of Yahweh in Isaiah from the Old Testament, and finally the Gospels and wider references outside of these in the New Testament.

THE BOOK OF JOB

Girard admits that the mimetic cycle that produces the scapegoat mechanism is to be found only partially in the Old Testament.[45] The "mimetic crisis" and collective violence parts of the cycle are

---

40. Mack, "Innocent Transgressor," 145.
41. Mack, "Innocent Transgressor," 163.
42. Hom, "Girard for the Uninitiated," 5.
43. Kirwan, "Rene Girard," 206.
44. Knott, "God of Victims," 407.
45. Girard, *I See Satan Fall*, 106.

most certainly there, and these he treats in his most extensive analysis of the Old Testament texts in his short book *Job: The Victim of His People*.[46] Girard sees the uniqueness of Job in its confrontation with two conceptions of God. On the one hand is a God of persecutors, represented by the hostile crowd, who by occasion of mimetic whim have turned against Job; on the other is the God of victims, represented by Job's affirmation of the deity.[47] Girard points out that in Job 17:6–10, Job is able to recognize how as a victim he has united an unjustly hostile crowd against him, and that really what he is protesting is the scapegoat mechanism and his being made the scapegoat. Job's friends initially try to console him but later threaten him with harsh and violent words, becoming part of the persecutors and projecting the collective expression of the violence of the community onto God (Job 15:20–23; 20:22–29). Job resists this murderous conformity of the multitude and is finally able to defeat this mimetic contagion by insisting on his innocence and his appeal to the God of victims that is on his side, affirming, "For I know that my Redeemer lives, and at last he will stand upon the earth" (Job 19:25). Girard descries this text as alluding to a skepticism of mimetic violence, the like of which no mythical story had ever demonstrated. He sees a compelling difference between the Bible and myth in that it is only in the Bible that there existed a questioning of the guilt of the victims of collective community violence.[48]

Against this somewhat convincing reading of Job, biblical commentaries relay the traditional interpretation of Job as a man who, in the midst of great suffering, though he has done nothing to deserve it, submits humbly to the divine will and shows consistent courage and patience, notwithstanding his protestations of innocence. According to this view, there was no solution to the problem of Job; he simply had to have faith and in the end was justified by God.[49] Baruch Levine, writing in 1985, found no evidence

46. Frear, "René Girard on Mimesis," 122.
47. Girard, *I See Satan Fall*, 117.
48. Girard, *I See Satan Fall*, 118.
49. Fuller, *New Catholic Commentary*, 417–20.

in Job of the Girardian interpretation that Job was being made a scapegoat for his community. Perhaps harshly, he accuses Girard of a "disdainful attitude towards the role of languages in the interpretation of ancient classics" and furthermore finds Girard guilty of extracting from the book of Job those parts that epitomize his own concerns.[50] He does not find any link between the suffering of Job and the well-being of the community, which is present in the scapegoat argument. Rather, he sees the story of Job as a challenge to the doctrine that the unfortunate must have offended God and that the innocents are never punished by a just God. Job is rejected by his community in the same way that society sometimes tends to blame the unfortunate for their own downfall. In this light Job was a heroic dissident to this hardening of attitudes.[51] If this is the case, then it raises very difficult questions for the person of faith as to the relation between God, who is seen to be in control of all things, and the suffering of righteous people, a theme that Jeremiah alluded to as well (Jer 12:1). Nevertheless, Levine is adamant that Job is not a scapegoat in the sense that the suffering servant in Isaiah might be said to represent.[52]

THE SUFFERING SERVANT OF YAHWEH

Those who have taken on the work of Girard and engaged in a thorough biblical exegetical analysis (which Girard had encouraged from the outset of his work with biblical texts) have emphasized the biblical defense of victims throughout the Old Testament, in particular the psalms of lament and the texts of the prophets. Psalm 31:14–18, for example, tells of a persecuted victim being encircled by a murderous collective and screaming his cries of despair into the air for God to avenge the violence they were made to suffer. Girard would see the significance of this in terms of biblical revelation—the drawing of attention to the plight of the

---

50. Levine, "René Girard on Job," 126.
51. Levine, "René Girard on Job," 131–33.
52. Levine, "René Girard on Job," 128.

victim and the allusion to a vengeful God that they cry out to for support—as traces of myth.[53] The suffering servant of Yahweh in Isa 53 is seen by Girard as a paradigmatic scapegoat that climaxes the Old Testament's revelation of the God who is on the side of victims and foretells the suffering of the Messiah in strikingly similar terms: scorned, beaten, and condemned by his fellow man (Isa 53:2–3). The decisive passages, though, are those that stress the innocence of the servant—"although he had done no violence, and there was no deceit in his mouth" (Isa 53:9)—and those that make it clear that the people were principally responsible for his death, negating any suggestion that God bore any responsibility (Isa 53:4–5).[54] Girard here makes a compelling case that this text rejects the scapegoat mechanism altogether.

It is in this last point, though, that much biblical scholarship diverges from Girard's attempts to portray the suffering servant as part of the biblical revelation and exposition of the scapegoat mechanism. By way of contrast, they point out that the text relates the servant suffering intensely to expiate the sins of other men and bring health and salvation to sinners through his pain. The suffering that the servant, through humility and gentleness, endures is not to be seen as a sign of the sinfulness of the sufferer but rather as a substitutionary atonement where he carries the burden for the sins of others.[55] In this way Isaiah is seen to be interpreting the death of the servant as a guilt offering (Isa 53:10). This has allusions to the guilt offering in Lev 5:15–19 and the sacrificing of a ram without defect. According to Isaiah, the servant is "like a lamb" (Isa 53:7) who takes the place of Israel and is wounded and crushed (Isa 53:5, 11–12) to suffer the fate that they deserved as a result of their rebellion against God.[56]

Girard himself was not blind to the indications in this text that pointed towards a substitutionary view of atonement arising from Isaiah's suffering servant. He claimed that the work of exegesis

---

53. Palaver, *René Girard's Mimetic Theory*, 209.
54. Girard, *Things Hidden*, 151.
55. Fuller, *New Catholic Commentary*, 594–95.
56. Thielman, "Atonement," 107–8.

was ongoing in precisely the opposite direction to associating God with requiring a violent sacrifice to appease his wrath. Rather, an explanation of the Old Testament would not be complete without recognizing it in accordance with the full revelation of Christ and his exposing of the scapegoat mechanism in the Gospels. Girard saw the prophetic books as increasingly divesting the violent characteristics of primitive deities that were mistakenly attributed to Yahweh, but he had to admit that it was impossible to arrive at a conception of God in the Old Testament that was entirely foreign to violence.[57]

One of those who took to continuing the work of exegesis on the Old Testament was a Swiss Jesuit, Raymond Schwager, who became one of the strongest defenders and advocates of Girard's system of work. He was credited with finding a much more convincing exegetical underpinning for Girard's work based on his approach to biblical texts.[58] Schwager found that there existed one thousand cases where violence is attributed directly to Yahweh and a hundred passages where Yahweh gives an express command to others to kill people, and concluded it was necessary to qualify God's violence as irrational in some of these instances (e.g., Exod 4:24–26).[59] Yet, he brought a Girardian witness to bear on this by finding in the Old Testament the gradual emergence of a community of peace and love breaking out in the midst of these misinterpreted instances of divine violence.[60]

THE GOSPELS AND THE WIDER NEW TESTAMENT

It is precisely in the passion accounts of the New Testament that the Gospels reveal a truth already partially disclosed in the Old Testament, according to Girard. Biblical revelation has found

---

57. Girard, *Things Hidden*, 151.
58. North, "Violence and the Bible," 16.
59. Schwager, *Must There Be Scapegoats*, 47–67.
60. Schwager, *Must There Be Scapegoats*, 135.

its culmination in the Christ event of the New Testament.[61] The passion narratives are therefore used by Girard to describe a non-sacrificial reading of the death of Christ that puts it in stark opposition to any interpretation of Jesus' death as a satisfaction theory of atonement, as this would go against the very scapegoating mechanism that the Gospels seek to subvert and expose.

The key to Girard's interpretation of the New Testament is that Jesus refused to become involved in the spiral of violence and revealed God as a God of nonviolence. In making this argument, he has made some dramatic claims that New Testament exegetes have missed the true message of Jesus from the earliest Christian times, including those who formulated the New Testament itself. Other biblical scholars have praised Girard for allowing obscure texts to regain their meaning—and others to take on a new meaning in relation to the whole.[62] For example Girard uses John 10:18 ("No one takes it [my life] from me, but I lay it down of my own accord") in illustrating Jesus' refusal to be a part of the domination system fueled by sacrificial violence. In Matt 9:13, Jesus invokes Hosea explicitly rejecting the cult of sacrifice upon which the Pharisees had understood the Jewish religion, stating, "I desire mercy, and not sacrifice." This position leaves Jesus with a formidable coalition of enemies, and he doesn't help himself when he describes them as allies with Satan, who was a murderer from the beginning and the father of lies (John 8:44). Girard claims that Jesus sees through the scapegoat mechanism that has held societies together in a false peace since the earliest times and calls out those who seek to perpetuate it for their own ends. This coalition of worldly powers then unites, intent that one man should die for the people so that the nation should not perish (John 11:50). Girard relates how Luke in his passion account describes the coming together of onetime enemies, Herod and Pilate, as a characteristic reconciliation that a collective murder brings about (Luke 23:12).[63] Mimetic contagion sweeps across the crowd at Jesus' trial to the point where

---

61. Girard, *I See Satan Fall*, 130.
62. North, "Violence and the Bible," 18.
63. Girard, *I See Satan Fall*, 132.

even his most passionate follower, Peter, abandons him by denying him three times in the temple of the high priests (Mark 14:54) and the whole of the people demand his crucifixion (Matt 27:22, 25). Schwager summarizes it well:

> Ultimately all those elements which Girard in his ethnological and anthropological analyses identified and summarized as the scapegoat mechanism are at play in the condemnation of Jesus (the ganging together of all against one, the violent discharge, self-deception, transference of guilt onto the victim of collective violence).[64]

The texts differ crucially, though, from those of myths in that they are written from the point of view of the persecuted victim who is completely innocent. Girard uses John 15:25, "They hated me without cause," as a key passage for understanding that Jesus is recognized by the New Testament writers as a falsely accused scapegoat.[65]

Without doubt, Girard presents a very convincing case for his theory in his use of the Gospel texts. He also credits Paul, with whom he has had a difficult relationship to say the least, with recognizing that Christ "disarmed the principalities and powers and made a public example of them, triumphing over them in him" (Col 2:14–15), and in doing so reduced mythology to powerlessness by exposing its violent contagion.[66] Girard shows how Paul contributes to the *Christus Victor* perspective on the atonement by quoting his letter to the Corinthians: "None of the rulers of this age understood this [the hidden wisdom of God]; for if they had, they would not have crucified the Lord of glory" (1 Cor 2:8). The rulers of this age here correlate to Satan, who had hoped that the victim mechanism as employed against Christ would function as usual, free from any suspicions, and get rid of Jesus and his message. However, the unexpected outcome in the resurrection reversed the violent contagion that had overcome Jesus' disciples, and it was

---

64. Schwager, "Christ's Death," 116.
65. Palaver, *René Girard's Mimetic Theory*, 208.
66. Girard, *I See Satan Fall*, 138.

they who broadcast the passion accounts to the world and gave light to the secret that had held people in darkness.[67] In this sense, Girard praised Origen and many of the Greek fathers' thesis of "Satan duped by the Cross," a victim of some kind of divine ruse. He maintained that their understanding of revelation became obscured because the anthropology of the Cross remains obscured, and this is where he sees his work as ultimately beneficial.[68]

THE CONFLICT WITH THE "SATISFACTION" VIEW OF ATONEMENT

Against Girard's thesis, any number of biblical scholars have lined up to criticize him, especially in respect to the New Testament texts that point towards a satisfaction theory of atonement. For proponents of the substitution/satisfaction theory of atonement, the outright rejection of Jesus' death as a sacrifice to satisfy the wrath of God against his sinful people is simply not a logical position to take given its prominence in many places in the Bible.[69] In response, which many biblical scholars and theologians see as justifying their condemnations of Girard's perceived arrogance, Girard posits a certain unawareness of the scapegoat mechanism among the authors of the New Testament themselves, which accounts for any time they appear to describe Jesus' death as atonement for sins to please the just wrath of God. He accounts for their inability to understand all that was at work in the Christ event as giving them greater credibility and claims that they were able to articulate the Jesus story as well as they did because they were under control of the intelligence of Jesus.[70]

---

67. Girard, *I See Satan Fall*, 149.
68. Girard, *I See Satan Fall*, 152.
69. Girard, *I See Satan Fall*, 123.
70. Girard, *Scapegoat*, 163.

IMPLICATIONS FOR THE CHRISTIAN LIFE

What is compelling, though, about Girard's work is how he ties difficult teachings of Jesus together with the uncovering of the scapegoat mechanism as the complete repudiation on which all sacrificial theologies are built, saying that from this the nonviolence of God is revealed. In what he considers as central to the New Testament texts, the Sermon on the Mount describes Jesus' rejection of all forms of interpersonal violence, reaching its climax in the command to love one's enemy (Matt 5:43–45).

Jesus' message about the kingdom of God is portrayed as a genuine message of salvation in terms of an eschatological soteriology and a complete break from the violence that binds societies together under the spell of a myth about the need for redemptive violence. Jesus is the Son of God, free of violence from the very beginning and committed to establishing God's radical nonviolence in a culture rooted in violence.[71] Girard's theory serves to bolster prophetic biblical scholarship supporting the imitation of Jesus' revelation of God as nonviolent, neatly summed up by John L. McKenzie: "Jesus taught that violence belongs to the Reign of Satan, and that men must expel violence if they wish to liberate themselves from the Reign of Satan."[72]

FOLLOWING JESUS IN NONVIOLENCE

The new commandment that Jesus gave his disciples on the night before he was murdered is key to discerning how a Christian should live his or her life. Loving as Jesus loved is the simple but difficult instruction that Jesus left his followers to practice in their individual and collective lives. It is this Christlike love in action, no matter how small and insignificant it may seem, that builds the kingdom of God. Gospel nonviolence is the central component of this love, and its implications for the social, political, and economic lives of Christians are in total contrast to the ways of the world.

71. Palaver, *René Girard's Mimetic Theory*, 209.
72. McKenzie, *New Testament Without Illusion*, 33.

While there is not scholarly unanimity that Jesus taught an ethic of nonviolence for his followers to imitate, there is a growing scholarly consensus that nonviolence lay at the heart of Jesus' teaching and practice. It is very normal for biblical scholars to debate the many themes and ideas that are found in the Scriptures, but when it comes to debating the centrality of gospel nonviolence in the Christian faith, the evidence is overwhelming. The Sermon on the Mount, with its emphasis of love even towards those considered enemies, is seen to lie at the center of the Christian moral revolution and, as such, has much for Christians today to reflect on. Far from proposing an individualistic ethic for achieving a greater degree of piety, Jesus' teachings and practice of nonviolence were a risky but real alternative to the ways of the world characterized by domination and all kinds of social, economic, and political oppression. Jesus' execution was made necessary for the political and religious authorities of the time because of the real threat that his message posed for the established order.[73] Girard's work emphasizes that the nonviolent kingdom of God, embodied in the life and teaching of Jesus, ultimately triumphs over the violent powers of the world under Satan's dominion through the paradoxical victory of the cross and the resurrection.

By a willingness to fully imitate Christ in love and witness to the truth, the Christian was called to embrace public suffering and persecution for the sake of the Gospel and the construction of the new kingdom, present in the now but fully established in the future. This was a call that became embodied in the lives of many known and unknown Christians in the early centuries of the church, which will be discussed in chapter 2.

---

73. Yoder, *Politics of Jesus*, 49.

2

Early Christianity and Active Nonviolence

FOR THE FIRST THREE centuries of Christianity as it spread throughout the Roman Empire, the early church set itself up as an active opponent of pagan society and in its liberating praxis had a very deep social and political potency. The practice of nonviolence as taught by Jesus was taken as a given for building the kingdom of God, and the lives of the apologists and martyrs during this period bear testimony to the fact that gospel teaching on peacemaking was taken seriously.[1] This chapter will explore some of the evidence for this assertion and look at how the adoption of the Christian religion by the Roman Empire had far-reaching negative consequences for the dissemination and practice of gospel nonviolence stretching to the present day.

---

1. Musto, *Catholic Peace Tradition*, 34.

THE APOLOGISTS AND GOSPEL-INSPIRED NONVIOLENCE

The intellectual tradition of the apologists during this period is evidence that love of enemies in imitation of Christ was to be part of daily practice rather than the temptation to imitate the savageness of their persecutors. Justin Martyr (ca. 100–ca. 165), who died during the persecutions of Marcus Aurelius, was one example of this tradition who claimed in his writings that Christians, having been converted from war and violence, were to turn their swords into plowshares and "cultivate piety, justice and love of mankind."[2] Later, Tertullian (ca. 160–ca. 220) would coin the famous phrase, "When Christ disarmed Peter, He disarmed every soldier."[3] Hippolytus (ca. 160–ca. 236) is credited with writings forbidding Christians in the Roman Church from entering into occupations that employ violence: "A soldier of the civil authority must be taught not to kill men and refuse to do so if he is commanded."[4] Cyprian, the bishop of Carthage, consistently reminded his congregations that killing ranked with adultery and deceit as a mortal sin and the one who kills was to be excommunicated from the church.[5]

Although it is undeniable that evidence exists for Christians serving in the Roman army during these first three centuries, it must be seen against the context of the overall commitment of the early church to nonviolence in word and deed. The numbers in the army were undoubtedly small given that the rural peasantry, who made up most of the recruits, were pagan even after the time of the Christian emperors and, being mainly city folk, Christians weren't exactly considered good material for army duty. While the refusal to swear oaths and offer sacrifices to the pagan gods of the empire was undoubtedly a factor in the Christian antipathy towards serving in the military, it is clear that adherence to the nonviolent

---

2. Musto, *Catholic Peace Tradition*, 35.
3. Musto, *Catholic Peace Tradition*, 35.
4. Musto, *Catholic Peace Tradition*, 36.
5. Musto, *Catholic Peace Tradition*, 37.

teachings of Christ was of primary importance in the decision not to fight.

MARTYRDOM IN THE EARLY CHURCH

Of the so-called "soldier saints" who suffered martyrdom, Maximilian (274–295) is one of the best known and serves as an example of a Christian who refused to fight in times of active military crisis. Having been drafted into the army by his father, Maximilian revealed that he was a Christian and stated his refusal to fight for this world as he belonged to the army of God.[6] Maximilian was condemned and executed as a result of his loyalty to the nonviolent Jesus. Maximilian and other soldiers who refused to kill provide evidence that, of the small number of Christians who did serve in the Roman army, their service usually involved peaceful police-type work, and their over-riding testimony was loyalty to nonviolence as the way of the new kingdom. It was not until Athanasius, writing after the time of Constantine in the Eastern Imperial Church, that any evidence appears of specific approval of Christians serving in the army, praise for their warrior qualities, or any formulations of a theology of war.[7]

Rather, martyrdom was seen as an exhortation of the kingdom of God. The active opposition of the early Christians to the imperial cult led Rome to view this strange group of people, who had formed an illegal organization, as having a set of attitudes that struck at the very heart of the fabric of the empire.[8] The danger of this growing religion was recognized and evidenced in the persecution brought upon the early church. The history of Christian martyrdom from these earliest times was a witness of their faithfulness to the nonviolent teachings of Jesus. The ideal of nonviolence was enshrined in the willingness of the martyrs to give public witness to the truth of the lordship of Christ and suffer death for

---

6. Musto, *Catholic Peace Tradition*, 41–43.
7. Musto, *Catholic Peace Tradition*, 42–43.
8. Musto, *Catholic Peace Tradition*, 39.

it in faithfulness to Christ's command to love their enemies. Furthermore, in an ironic twist of fate, it was viewed as the single most important factor in the transformation of the Roman world as individual conversion gave way to institutional change.[9]

THE CONSTANTINIAN SHIFT AND THE BEGINNING OF THE JUST WAR TRADITION

Commonly known as the "Constantinian shift," the "conversion" of the Emperor Constantine and the beginning of the Christian Roman Empire had a profound impact on the faithfulness of the early church to the nonviolent teachings of Christ as the way of the new kingdom. The battle that triggered the series of changes took place at Milvian Bridge, which crossed the River Tiber, when Constantine, having been declared emperor in 306, took on a pretender to the throne in 312. The first two letters in Christ's name in Greek appeared as a monogram on the shields of his troops, following a supposed vision of a cross of light in the sky. The crushing victory that followed encouraged Constantine in his further battles for supremacy to order his troops to say a prayer to the God of the Christians to enable success. His favoring of Christianity led not only to a declaration of toleration and subsequent halting of the persecution of Christians, ratified in what we now call the Edict of Milan in 313, but also to the lavishing of great wealth and status on leading members of the church.[10]

The fusion of church leaders into positions of imperial authority saw the church take on the trappings of the empire, with the Roman administrative building, the basilica, becoming the model Christian church and a church hierarchy emerging that was modeled on Roman imperial bureaucracy.[11] The title of the bishop of Rome rose in status due to Rome being the capital of the empire, and with this it became a role that gradually went on to replace the

---

9. Musto, *Catholic Peace Tradition*, 45.
10. MacCulloch, *History of Christianity*, 189–91.
11. Musto, *Catholic Peace Tradition*, 46–47.

Early Christianity and Active Nonviolence

Roman emperor in the West. With Christianity becoming the official religion of the empire, a large number of superficial converts were brought into its ranks, and it was ruled that only Christians could be allowed to serve in the army.[12] A new ethic on peace was therefore needed that could justify violence as a means of defending the Christian empire and thus the achievement of peace. This was to become known as the "Christian just war theory," despite having zero basis in Jesus' teachings and revelation of God. It has, however, been a massive influence on Christian thought in regard to issues of war and peace ever since.

The work of Saint Augustine of Hippo (354–430) in *The City of God* was defining in terms of articulating a just war theory based mainly on the pagan theories of Cicero and other Roman thinkers. This was composed in response to the charge of Volusian, after the sack of Rome by the Visigoths in 410, that a still active belief of Christians in nonviolence was responsible for the ruin of the empire. Augustine postulated that it was possible to love an enemy internally and still kill him, positing the idea of peace as a dichotomy between the inner tranquility of the Christian and the demands of society, which sometimes necessitate the need to wage war. Inner peace could be facilitated by order based on force, so long as the force was based on motivations of love. Despite his admiration for Rome as an agent for peace and fellowship he did nevertheless critique the violence and exploitation inherent in the empire and lamented the occasion for any wars to take place. He believed that true justice and peace were not to be found within kingdoms of this world that were simply "gangs of criminals on a large scale." Rather, these were brought about only through the love of God and the love of all people, which constituted the city of God sojourning in this world of sin until the new Jerusalem is established at the end times.[13] Despite other Christian intellectuals in the East like Gregory of Nyssa, who emphasized Christian differences with the empire and a rejection of war that was to become a strong tradition in Byzantine history, there was just enough

---

12. Musto, *Catholic Peace Tradition*, 47.
13. Musto, *Catholic Peace Tradition*, 49.

ambiguity in Augustine's work on the issue of war and peace to lead to the just war theory becoming one of the most influential collection of ideas in Christian history, leading to the widespread departure from Jesus' teachings on nonviolence that went with it.[14]

Walter Wink, in the last book of his trilogy on the "powers," *Engaging the Powers*, gave a devastating critique of the origin of the just war theory in Christian thought. He viewed the weapon-less victory of Christianity over the Roman Empire as having occasioned the weaponless victory of the empire over the gospel. This shift was catastrophic for a faith that was rooted in its critique of a dominative social order in favor of a vision of a nonviolent one, as it meant an embracing and rationalization of oppression. Augustine's work on the just war, drawing from Stoic principles, enabled the intellectual accommodation of Christianity to its new status as a privileged religion in support of the state.[15]

A big problem for the church in the adoption of this "just war" outlook was that very few Christians had ever been taught, and hence were unable, to articulate the nuances of what was a theory based on very specific and rigorous criteria embedded in a very complex ethical discipline. Historically, Wink pointed out, no authoritative Christian body prior to the commencement of hostilities had ever decreed that one side or the other was justified in their warfare by virtue of just war criteria.[16] He saw that the adherence to redemptive violence that perpetuated the domination system was deeply ingrained in society but that the church had a vocation for nonviolence grounded in the teachings of Jesus, which revealed the nature of God and the ethos of the kingdom. He was adamant that the "removal of nonviolence from the gospel blasted the keystone from the arch, and Christianity collapsed into a religion of personal salvation."[17]

Other authors on the period in question are much less scathing in their analyses of the Constantinian shift and its consequences

14. Musto, *Catholic Peace Tradition*, 50.
15. Wink, *Engaging the Powers*, 212.
16. Wink, *Engaging the Powers*, 213.
17. Wink, *Engaging the Powers*, 217.

for the church. British theologian Oliver O'Donovan attempted, in his book *The Desire of the Nations*, to counter the image of Christendom after the Constantinian shift as a period of darkness for the church and its faithfulness to its God-given mission in the world. While he critiqued the enthusiastic praise of Eusebius (bishop of Caesarea from 313 to 339) for Constantine as exaggerated, he shared Eusebius's view that the essential factor in the Constantinian moment was the victory of God. With the word of truth and the blood spilled by the martyrs, the pagan empire had yielded to the army of Christ.[18] While not at all constituting the parousia, those who ruled thereafter in Christendom and those who thought and argued about government were, in O'Donovan's view, for the most part people of faith who believed the gospel to be true. As such, he argued, it is important for Christians today to learn lessons from a Christendom that has long since disappeared as opposed to blaming it for all the ills the church has got caught up in since Constantine.[19]

American theologian Peter J. Leithart, for his part, mounted a defense of the reputation of Constantine against theologians like Stanley Hauerwas and John Yoder, whom he accused of promoting a popular image of Constantine as a murderous, tyrannical, hardened politician who never really became Christian but used the energy of the church for his own political ends.[20] Rather, he believed Constantine to be the first overtly Christian emperor, whose reign, far from signaling the fall of the church, represented a model for Christian political practice and showed what good Christian government looked like.[21] Leithart argued that one of Constantine's greatest achievements was to "eliminate sacrifice from Roman life."[22] However, this did not extend to the sacrificing of human blood in wars and the maintaining of political order

---

18. O'Donovan, *Desire of the Nations*, 193–98.
19. O'Donovan, *Desire of the Nations*, 194.
20. Leithart, *Defending Constantine*, 10.
21. Leithart, *Defending Constantine*, 201.
22. Leithart, *Defending Constantine*, 327.

with lethal violence, which was far from conformity with Jesus' teaching and life example of nonviolence.

While defenders of the church's embrace of political power after Constantine point to certain biblical treatments of political terms like sovereignty, authority, judgment, and justice to back up their positive assessment, the commandment of Jesus to love one another as he had loved required that Christians adopt the ethic of Jesus' nonviolence in every aspect of their lives. Therein lies the strongest argument for Wink and others in their negative analysis of what the Constantinian shift meant for the church in the centuries to come. Gospel nonviolence undoubtedly lay at the heart of the practice of the early church, as the evidence shows. It was without question a relief to all in the church when Constantine ordered Christianity to be tolerated and the persecution to end, but as Wink and others have pointed out, the church's embrace of the empire saw its radical edge blunted.

Much of what has been written on the events after this comes down to whether one sees nonviolence prohibiting Christians from participating in the kind of violent practices that the state requires to survive in a violent world or whether one chooses to rationalize Christian involvement in violence-justifying political institutions and downplay the ethical demands of the gospel for living out a nonviolent life in imitation of Christ. Theologians for the most part are split along these lines, and most have decided that the debate on gospel nonviolence as a Christian duty is not worth writing about. What follows, though, is a snippet of some of the theology that takes gospel nonviolence seriously and does not shy away from placing it at the center of the Christian revolution.

3

Theologians and the Nonviolent Revolution of Jesus

> We have tried to produce a form of Christianity that will be tolerable to those who believe that the best way to deal with your enemies is to beat their heads in. And, we have done this. We have produced the Christian ethic of the just war. This is not the New Testament [apostolic Christianity], and every theologian knows it.[1]
>
> —JOHN L. MCKENZIE

THE BROAD CHRISTIAN ACCEPTANCE of the justification of the use of violence and war that resulted from the Roman Empire's adoption of Christianity as its official religion characterized much of the church's history as Christians gained access to and responsibility for government and political power. It went as far as generating a crusade ideology, where the violent capture of the Holy Land was claimed to be serving the gospel itself. Augustine's work was also adapted by Aquinas into a more developed just war theory in the

---

1. McKenzie, *Myths and Realities*, 30–31.

Middle Ages. Aquinas believed that the imitation of Christ on the altar necessitated that clergy embody the nonviolent teachings of Jesus, but war to defend the common good within carefully defined limits was acceptable for non-ordained Christians to engage in.[2] Given the undoubted intellectual genius of Aquinas and the fact that most Christians up to that point in history and beyond were illiterate, there was bound to be reluctance to challenge someone like him in matters of theology. This reluctance among theologians to criticize Aquinas for his extraordinary claim that the ordained clergy were to live by different Christian ethics than the laity in matters of war continues to the present day. Nevertheless, there were many examples of individuals like Saint Francis of Assisi and Erasmus, along with peace movements such as the "Truce of God," that continued to promote the nonviolent approach to Christian peacemaking into the modern era.[3]

One of the most devastating critiques of justified violence, particularly of the state, came from Leo Tolstoy, known otherwise for his massive literary achievements. He did, however, write a few very influential books—among them, *The Kingdom of God Is Within You*—that inspired people like Dorothy Day, Gandhi, and Martin Luther King Jr. in their nonviolent praxis throughout the decades that followed. Tolstoy argued that modern states legitimize violence through their military, police, and legal structures and that as such, a Christian could play no part in them.

> Governments not only do not renounce violence but cannot do so; for government means violence, organization of violence.[4]

His spiritual awakening led him to embrace Christianity as a religion of nonviolence and love in which the Christian was called to renounce all violence. Instead the Christian was to enact social change through moral transformation and nonviolent resistance.

---

2. Cahill, "Traditional Catholic Thought," 106.
3. Butigan and Dear, "Catholic Practice of Nonviolence," 129–30.
4. Tolstoy, *Kingdom of God*, 36.

His depiction of war was particularly prophetic and insightful given what was to come in World War I:

> And, drowning in their hearts their despair by means of songs, debauchery, and vodka, hundreds of thousands of simple, good people, torn away from peaceful labor, from their wives, mothers, children, will march, with weapons of murder in their hands, whither they will be driven. They will go to freeze, to starve, to be sick, to die from diseases, and finally they will arrive at the place where they will be killed by the thousand, and they will kill by the thousand, themselves not knowing why, men whom they have never seen and who have done them and can do them no harm.
>
> And when there shall be collected so many sick, wounded, and killed that nobody will have the time to pick them up, and when the air shall already be so infected by this rotting food for cannon that even the authorities will feel uncomfortable, then they will stop for a while, will somehow manage to pick up the wounded, will haul off and somewhere throw into a pile the sick, and will bury the dead, covering them with lime, and again they will lead on the whole crowd of the deceived, and will continue to lead them on in this manner until those who have started the whole thing will get tired of it, or until those who needed it will get what they needed.
>
> And again will men become infuriated, brutalized, and bestialized, and love will be diminished in the world, and the incipient Christianization of humanity will be delayed for decades and for centuries. And again will the people, who gain thereby, begin to say with assurance that, if there is a war, this means that it is necessary, and again they will begin to prepare for it the future generations, by corrupting them from childhood.[5]

Tolstoy's description of war, and of the process of brutalization that precedes and follows it, was accurately played out in the two world wars that he did not live to see in the twentieth century. It is an incredibly insightful and devastating critique of

---

5. Tolstoy, "Christianity and Patriotism," 449.

how ordinary people are essentially tricked into doing things they would never have considered themselves capable of doing to their fellow human beings and how easily they fall for the lies of the powerful and end up becoming disciples of political and economic mass murderers, rather than the nonviolent Jesus.

The horror of the twentieth century, in which an unparalleled number of people in human history were killed in wars that continue to persist in the present century has meant that theologians have had to continually grapple with Christian approaches to peacemaking. While the predominant view still holds that violence is an unfortunate but realistic necessity in a world of sin to bring about justice in a world where injustice is so prevalent, there have been a great many theologians who have arrived at very different conclusions and in doing so have brought back to the spotlight the focus on Jesus' teachings on nonviolence as a realistic way of working for peace in the world.

In this chapter, I will briefly reference the contribution of Father John L. McKenzie as one of the most preeminent biblical scholars of his day who dedicated his life's work to articulating the scriptural basis for gospel nonviolence and how Christians are to take it seriously in their lives. Next, I will examine the work of Walter Rauschenbusch and the contribution he made to renewing the focus for theology in helping Christians embody the social, political, and economic ideals of the kingdom as lived and taught by Jesus. I will also analyze the insights of Ched Myers as to how Christians living in a situation of empire can bear witness to the radical nonviolent vision of the kingdom. Finally, I will explore the work of René Girard, in particular the apocalyptic character of his later work, as a hugely significant complement to the work of theologians.

JOHN L. MCKENZIE AND THE SCHOLARLY SHIFT TOWARDS GOSPEL NONVIOLENCE

The books of Father John L. McKenzie are among the most accessible and brilliantly articulated contributions to understanding the nonviolent teachings of Jesus from a scriptural point of view and how this becomes the centerpiece for Christian behavior in the world. For nearly two decades (ca. 1956–1975), he stood at the forefront of Catholic biblical scholarship. He served as president of the Catholic Biblical Association, became the first Catholic elected president of the International Society of Biblical Literature, and was the first Catholic appointed to the faculty of the University of Chicago Divinity School. As the sole author of the nine-hundred-thousand-word *Dictionary of the Bible*, along with hundreds of other books and scholarly articles, he was by any academic standard among the finest biblical scholars of his time. Yet, he was concerned that the new insights into the Gospels enabled by the modern instruments of biblical research would remain in the ivory towers of academic theology if he didn't accept the intellectual and professional risks inherent in presenting new, neglected, or controversial insights from the foundational texts of Christianity to both the scholarly world and the broader public.

Father McKenzie firmly believed that the gospel must be critically engaged with the moral and spiritual crises of its historical moment. To preach Christ while ignoring the concrete evils of the twentieth century, in his view, was to betray the very message of Christ. McKenzie would not allow himself to be complicit in such silence and so left his readers in no doubt about the true nature of God as revealed by Jesus and what that entailed for Christian living. He made it abundantly clear that Jesus rejected violence totally and that his followers were to do the same. Any justification of violence had to be found outside of the teachings of Jesus in the Gospels. McKenzie believed the church should resist aligning with state power or embracing violence, instead embodying a transformative, countercultural kingdom rooted in service, peace, and radical allegiance to Christ. For him, Christianity and the modern state were fundamentally incompatible. In his final work, *The Civilization of Christianity*, he delivered a stark verdict: "There is a deadly and irreconcilable opposition between western civilization and Christianity, and . . . one of them must destroy the other."[6] He argued that the pursuit of wealth, political authority, and the endorsement of violence are fundamentally incompatible with Jesus' teachings.

Despite the predominant thought within the circles of the church lending itself to reasoning against doing what was the Christian thing to do, Father McKenzie was unequivocal that Jesus really did mean for his followers to live out his teachings in the world, despite the cost that this could bring.

> If the Christian is true to his Christian love, it may kill him, impoverish him, or disgrace him. In any hypothesis he is sure to lose at least some of those goods of this world which Jesus took some trouble to point out are of no importance.[7]

This was a suffering born out of Christian love; however, it was quite distinct from the idea that suffering was pleasing to God, as some of the Christian aesthetics had it, whereby inflicting pain on themselves or denying themselves pleasure was seen as bringing them closer to Jesus. Rather, identification with Jesus' suffering was identification with Jesus' loving.[8] The power of love was seen in the death of Jesus and more fully in his resurrection. Death marked the end of one life and one world, whereas the resurrection inaugurated a new life and a new creation. In the resurrection, a new world was born, one in which Jesus lives. The truly revolutionary dimension of the Christian mystery is the enduring presence of God's love in Jesus Christ, the ongoing presence of the divine power first made manifest in the incarnation. Through this power, according to McKenzie, every person has been enabled, in any circumstance, to live the life of Jesus and to embody the love that redeems. The resurrection stands as the climax of God's saving act.[9]

---

6. McKenzie, *Civilization of Christianity*, 134.
7. McKenzie, *Power*, 232.
8. McKenzie, *Power*, 103.
9. McKenzie, *Power*, 119–21.

Father McKenzie's eloquent style of writing meant that his influence did indeed reach the ordinary Christian in the pew. He inspired figures like Dorothy Day and Father Emmanuel Charles McCarthy, one of the most eloquent and knowledgeable speakers on the nonviolent Jesus. McKenzie's books are still in print and stand as a timely challenge to the institutional church to reform and renew itself to the radical witness of the power of nonviolent Christ-love in the world today.

WALTER RAUSCHENBUSCH AND THE SOCIAL GOSPEL

Restoring the challenge of the Gospels to the living out of the ideals of the kingdom of God as proclaimed by Jesus lay at the heart of the theology proposed by Walter Rauschenbusch in the late nineteenth century and early twentieth century. A Baptist theologian born in 1861 to German parents who had moved to New York, he witnessed the harsh realities of capitalist industrialization in the lives of the poor and working class in New York, especially during his first posting as a minister in 1886. This led him to develop the doctrine of the kingdom of God that would see Christians work towards a better social order than the one whose burning injustices affected him deeply.[10]

Rauschenbusch perceived in the social crises of his day an ideal opportunity for the disciples of Jesus to work for change in the social order so that it would better reflect the demands of the kingdom. The social crisis of the fundamentally unjust social and economic system that capitalism had produced needed to be countered by what he came to call the "Social Gospel." He surmised that there had been a demise of the kingdom of God as a central concept in Christian theology after the Constantinian shift and that the church needed to reconnect with the revolutionary teachings of Jesus in order to fulfill its prophetic calling, otherwise it would be complicit in propping up an unjust social order. While

10. Scott, "Kingdom Come," 160.

not blind to the human tendency for self-interest he nevertheless believed that the more individuals embodied and lived out the radical teachings of Christ, the more society would change for the better. Christians were called by Christ to carry out this work using nonviolent means and suffer for their witness if need be.[11]

Rauschenbusch's life's work culminated in his final publication, *A Theology for the Social Gospel*, produced in 1917, a year before his death. By that time he had been deserted by a lot of his liberal minister friends in the United States for his opposition to his country's participation in World War I, which he opposed not only because he was convinced that violence was incompatible with the teachings of Jesus but also because of the huge profits the capitalist war machine was making at the expense of the mass slaughter of human beings.[12] His insights into the motivations that governments have for war are still relevant, and they resonate in the present time of mass communication and the propensity for getting out a pro-war message that people will believe. He cited the reality of human sinfulness as a reason to oppose wars given that the temptations of power and money lay behind so much of the world's conflicts despite the appeals of government leaders to the higher values of humanity.[13]

A later US theologian who was influenced by his work but came to reject his concept of the Social Gospel, Reinhold Niebuhr, disputed this depiction of reality as much too optimistic. Niebuhr contended that the reality of human sinfulness was the biggest reason why war was sometimes necessary and justifiable to pursue justice in this fallen world, and his self-styled Christian realist perspective came to be the dominant view among most Christians for the rest of the century.[14]

Rauschenbusch's work, though, cannot be dismissed as easily as Niebuhr and others would have it as being too utopian. He recognized that sin had both personal and social dimensions and

11. Rauschenbusch, *Revolutionary Christianity*, 87–88.
12. Scott, "Kingdom Come," 161.
13. Rauschenbusch, *Theology for the Social Gospel*, 74.
14. Scott, "Kingdom Come," 161.

that it was a failure of Classical Theology to understand the social aspect of sin, instead viewing sin almost exclusively as a private matter between God and the individual. Salvation from sin was to be found in the person turning away from selfishness and embracing cooperative work in solidarity with others to build the kingdom that Jesus proclaimed.[15] The kingdom of God would never be fully realized within the contingencies of human history but it could be progressively established with the cooperation between the human and divine, which would open the possibility of a much better social order than the one offered by capitalism.[16]

RESTORING THE KINGDOM OF GOD DOCTRINE TO THE CHURCH

In calling for the church to refocus the basis for its existence on the efforts to build the kingdom of God, Rauschenbusch's words could be seen as having relevance for the church today as it undergoes a period of deep reflection in light of the many scandals that have rocked it in the recent past. He postulated that the church had in effect moved up into the position of the supreme good in place of the concept of the kingdom, and that the ethical principles that Jesus taught that went along with this were lost as the promotion of the power of the church over rival political bodies was seen as promoting the supreme good of Christianity. The practices of lying, cheating, crime, and war were all used and justified when it came to playing this political game of increasing the power and wealth of the church.[17] He lamented that the lack of the kingdom idea led to the church becoming a conservative social influence in society, whereas the revolutionary force that it contains should have been at the forefront in movements for democracy and social justice. He did however remain hopeful that a renewed focus on the kingdom of God doctrine could give vitality back to theology

---

15. Rauschenbusch, *Theology for the Social Gospel*, 60.
16. Rauschenbusch, *Theology for the Social Gospel*, 145.
17. Rauschenbusch, *Theology for the Social Gospel*, 134.

and help the church recover a prophetic voice in the transfiguration of the social order, as well as individual souls.[18]

RAUSCHENBUSCH'S INFLUENCE ON STANLEY HAUERWAS

Walter Rauschenbusch's work was influential for later nonviolent theologians like Stanley Hauerwas, who shared his central idea of the kingdom of God as essential for an understanding of Christ and built on what he considered Rauschenbusch's deficient ecclesiology.[19] For Hauerwas, the kingdom of God was revealed in the person of Jesus through his relationship with God, and so it is possible to talk of Jesus in terms of the *autobasileia*, the "kingdom in person."[20] As the inaugurator of the kingdom, Jesus manifested its peaceable nature and set the example of nonviolent living that the Christian community must imitate in order to grow it. The nonviolent teachings of Jesus are therefore to be learned by Christians wishing to inhabit this kingdom.[21] He strongly argued that Christians are called to form a church that lives out the social ethic of Jesus as manifested in his life and teachings and to persevere with it until all are brought within his kingdom.[22] His theology therefore centers on how the growth of God's church is meant to witness to the nonviolent kingdom of God. In this sense he believed that "all theology must begin and end with ecclesiology."[23] The church, through the freedom that it receives in christological ecclesial nonviolence, is God's alternative to war. Adherence to the concrete demands of the kingdom involves peacemaking in a way that disturbs and challenges the false peace of the world built on coercive power rather than truth. This will most certainly involve

---

18. Rauschenbusch, *Theology for the Social Gospel*, 137.
19. Hauerwas, "Repent," 173–76.
20. Hauerwas, *Community of Character*, 45.
21. Hauerwas, *Peaceable Kingdom*, 72–95.
22. Hauerwas, *Peaceable Kingdom*, 42–44.
23. Hauerwas, *In Good Company*, 58.

hardship and even death for Christians who remain faithful to such an ethic in a world so intrinsically oriented to violence, but the good news of Christ's resurrection is the assurance that any martyrdom trusts itself in an eschatological way to the victory of God's eternal reign of peace.[24]

CHED MYERS AND RADICAL DISCIPLESHIP IN THE SITUATION OF EMPIRE

For US theologian and activist Ched Myers, the challenge facing Christians today, especially those in a first world setting, was returning to a theology and practice of radical discipleship. In Myers's stunning political reading of the Gospel of Mark in *Binding the Strong Man*, he demonstrated how Jesus lived and died resisting empire and renewing Israel's social vision. Critics point out that his point of view, in coming to the text with the model of liberation for peasants from oppression under a ruling elite, pervades and controls his whole analysis, in that he finds it everywhere, even when it might not be so in the opinion of other exegetes. Nevertheless, he is credited with a fresh approach to Mark, combining a narrative analysis with the use of social-scientific models.[25]

For Myers, the nonviolent cross of Jesus represented a "stumbling block" for political theologies insofar as the practices of revolutionary nonviolence so evident in the Gospels have been overlooked and marginalized by those who, seeking a politically engaged faith, subconsciously buy into the myth of what Walter Wink termed "redemptive violence."[26] Also of great concern for Myers was the tendency of some theological advocates of nonviolence to do such advocacy from a safe academic distance and not get involved in real struggles that need the radical witness of Jesus' active nonviolence.[27]

---

24. Thomson, *Ecclesiology of Stanley Hauerwas*, 186.
25. Rhoads, Review of *Binding*, 336.
26. Myers, *Binding the Strong Man*, 469.
27. Myers, "Confronting the Powers," 340.

Myers wrote his sequel to *Binding the Strong Man*, the book *Who Will Roll Away the Stone: Discipleship Queries for First World Christians*, as an exercise in theology to complement the exercise in exegesis found in his previous work. He concerned himself in this book with "exposing the roots of our socio-political and historical pathologies in the First World, and recovering the roots of our discipleship tradition."[28] He offered to do so from the perspective of someone living in the US—the *locus imperii* (the situation of empire), whose influence and reach is such that it forms the dominant culture in large swathes of the planet where Christians reside. He used the term "radical Christian discipleship" in full knowledge that the term "radical," meaning to go to the roots, was a demonized word in modern parlance and the term "discipleship" also wasn't particularly fashionable in a narcissistic capitalist world, given its demands for being a disciplined "follower."[29]

Central to Myers's theology was the idea of narrative shaping the convictions of believers. He claimed that the stories in Scripture that make up the narrative of biblical radicalism had been forgotten or seen as entertainment by "first world" Christians, while at the same time they had been seduced by the stories spun by the popular culture of the imperial propaganda machine. Worst still, Christians had confused their own stories with the narrative of empire and thus become expropriated into the service of oppression, which has manifested itself time and again throughout the history of the church since Constantine.[30] The task, then, was to reclaim the biblical tradition, face the illusions of the dominant culture with courage, and take heart from the history of the church, when Christians who took the stories of Scripture seriously were animated to repent, resist evil, and build a more humane world.[31]

The story from the biblical narrative most relevant for Myers in describing the historical narrative for "first world" Christians was that of the apostle Peter standing in the palace courtyard,

28. Myers, *Who Will Roll*, xxiii.
29. Myers, *Who Will Roll*, xxiii.
30. Myers, *Who Will Roll*, xxi.
31. Myers, *Who Will Roll*, xxii.

anguishing about his denial of Jesus. This was seen by Myers as a good starting point for theology in the *locus imperium*. Peter had followed Jesus at a distance (Mark 14:54) and managed to slip by the armed security of the high priest into the palace courtyard, where he was trying to fulfill his vow to follow Jesus to the end (Mark 14:29). Meanwhile, inside, Jesus was being tortured and interrogated for the supposed crime of heresy and treason. In a detail of significance for Myers, Peter was sitting with the guards, warming himself at their fire. Just at the moment when imperial justice was sentencing Jesus to the way of the cross, Peter was recognized and accused by a servant to the high priest of being an associate of Jesus (Mark 14:67). His subsequent denial in order to save his own skin was the denial of the consequences of discipleship that Jesus foretold in favor of an ignominious compromise of his true self.

For Myers this mirrors the struggle of the church in two millennia of the Christian era to faithfully follow Christ. In the *locus imperii* Christians have too often followed Jesus at a distance and warmed themselves at the imperial fire. According to Myers, it was only by looking again at the narrative of biblical radicalism that Christians could fight off the illness and death of denial and continue afresh the discipleship journey.[32]

DISMANTLING THE DOMINATION SYSTEM NONVIOLENTLY WITH SATYAGRAHA

The central revolutionary question in these times for Myers was how Christians dismantle the "domination system" that is characterized by a growing gulf between the rich and the poor, maintained only through the violence intrinsic to it.[33] While refusing to judge the morality of those who resort to violence as a quite reasonable response to situations of protracted injustice, particularly in crude settings in "developing" nations, Myers believed that solidarity with those on the receiving end of imperial oppression

---

32. Myers, *Who Will Roll*, 1–5.
33. Myers, *Who Will Roll*, 238.

didn't consist in ignoring the fact that Christians were called to live according to another law that necessitated nonviolent evangelical means to bring closer the reality of the kingdom. It was a mistake to claim that nonviolence belonged to a "developed world" setting because of the predominance of liberal democracies, and to say that armed struggle was justified in a "developing world" setting because of the more blatant violent repression there. A tradition of nonviolence had been forged in many "developing world" contexts, sometimes instead of armed struggle, like in Palestine, China, the Philippines, and South Africa, while inversely, violent resistance had been just as common in "developed world" contexts like the north of Ireland and the Basque Country.

In cautioning his followers against being stirred up when talk of war signaling the end times filled the air (Mark 13:7–8), Jesus, according to Myers, was critiquing the myth of war as a transformative practice. The spiral of violence, as brilliantly articulated by Brazilian Archbishop Dom Hélder Câmara, consisted of the established violence of injustice (violence no. 1), the violent revolt of the oppressed or youth fighting for a more just world (violence no. 2), and the repressive counterviolence of governmental authorities to quell revolution (violence no. 3). This classic scenario, all too familiar in human history, needed to be broken by a nonviolence that repudiates the gun.[34]

Myers credited theologian Jim Douglas with recognizing that the apocalyptic politics of Jesus could be best understood in modern terms by Gandhian nonviolence. This practice of satyagraha represented a hermeneutic key to understanding Mark's description of Jesus' invitation for his followers to "take up his cross" (Mark 8:34).[35] Myers understood this call of Jesus to be the central characteristic of discontinuity with the "domination system" and involved a vow of nonviolent resistance as a way of life.[36] This nonviolent struggle must resist the use of the means of the political economy of militarism that drives the domination system, but it must retain a militancy

34. Myers, *Who Will Roll*, 240–43.
35. Myers, *Who Will Roll*, 250–51.
36. Myers, *Who Will Roll*, 251.

that unmasks the structural characteristics of oppression and violence by confronting them publicly, in imitation of Jesus' confrontation with the powers.[37] Noncooperation and militant direct action were therefore, for Myers, essential aspects of this nonviolent resistance and served to bring out into the open much of the hidden violence generated by the unjust socioeconomic system. Myers cited examples of faith-based nonviolent resistance in the US from several decades of the twentieth century to illustrate this in action, among them Martin Luther King Jr.'s leadership of the Civil Rights Movement and the Witness for Peace group, which trained nonviolent observers to put their bodies into war zones like Nicaragua in the 1980s, not only to deter fighting and human rights abuses, but also to expose the covert US war on the Sandinistas. The courage and character shown by the people involved in these and other examples were of the type that Myers believed "developed world" Christians needed to follow in bearing witness to the nonviolent kingdom that Jesus calls his followers to live in.[38]

RENÉ GIRARD AND GOD'S NONVIOLENT ALTERNATIVE TO SACRIFICIAL RELIGION

In the modern era of technological advancement, humankind has created an unprecedented ability to enact mass killing. The work of René Girard, one of the twentieth century's most prominent theorists of culture, offers an enhanced anthropological understanding of Christianity and is of immense importance in comprehending how the nonviolence of Christianity is the key to freeing humankind from its own destruction.

As referenced previously, Girard's controversial theory on human nature and human culture stemmed from his analysis on classic literary texts that gradually unveiled what he termed "the romantic lie." This was a belief that human beings desire things or people based on our own internal desires, that our desires are

---

37. Myers, *Who Will Roll*, 254.
38. Myers, *Who Will Roll*, 257–60.

somehow autonomous. Girard came to the realization through reading the works of Dostoevsky, Cervantes, and Proust, among others, that human desire was in fact mediated through a third party, someone who we envy, admire, or imitate. This he called "mimetic" desire, which can lead to violence as competing rivals battle each other over desirable objects. To illustrate what he meant, Girard used the classic example of children and toys, which at first glance seems an entirely innocent scenario. If two children are in the same room with hundreds of toys, they would probably end up fighting each other over the same toy. This is because the toy has been given some kind of social value by one of the children because it is desired. The desire of the child who doesn't have it is mediated and reinforced by the desire of the other. A seemingly neutral environment of children playing can quickly become a scene of intense rivalry. The deeper implications of this mimetic desire on a societal scale are precisely where Girard expands his theory to explain the origins of human cultures and the birth of social dynamics.

As discussed earlier, Girard argued that early human societies, threatened by unending violence born of mimetic desire (imitation and rivalry), found stability through the scapegoat mechanism—uniting against and killing a chosen victim to restore peace. Over time, this act was ritualized, forming the basis of religion, sacrifice, and social order.[39]

The Gospels, Girard claims, expose and reverse this ancient pattern. In Jesus' crucifixion, the innocence of the victim is revealed, unveiling humanity's complicity in violence.[40] Though evil seems to triumph, it ultimately brings about its own defeat. The truly divine peace that Christ offered cannot be fully established without first depriving humankind of the peace that the world gives based on scapegoats. Christ's passion dismantles this false peace built on scapegoating and inaugurates a new, divine peace rooted in love, truth, and the Holy Spirit.[41]

39. McDonald, "Violence," 346–47.
40. Girard, *I See Satan Fall*, 142.
41. Girard, *I See Satan Fall*, 186.

Although Girard's compelling theories caused a lot of controversy when they first appeared in the 1980s, his work takes on an urgent focus in light of the violent political and environmental crisis that faces the world today.

"TOTAL" WAR AND THE COMING APOCALYPSE

In one of his final books before his death, *Battling to the End*, Girard explored the apocalyptic consequences of the contemporary historical and cultural setting as a hybrid one, in which some people have awareness of the scapegoat mechanism exposed in the gospel, while the same mechanism still continues to function.[42] The problem with this "in-between time" is the ever-accelerating drive of human-shaped history towards our own destruction in the guise of world wars, atomic weapons, multiple genocides, and climate disaster. Girard identified the transformation visible in the area of human conflict and warfare as having taken place at the time when nineteenth-century military theorist Carl von Clausewitz was writing, in the course of the Napoleonic wars, to a trend of "total war." This has negated the manner through which war was able to regulate and thus limit the violence arising from human rivalries and conflict. The "total" character of the wars of the twentieth century and the onset of technological advancements in ultimate weapons of mass destruction have unveiled a phenomenon of de-restricted and unlimited warfare constituting a properly "apocalyptic" phase of human history.[43]

Related to this proliferation of modern warfare, Girard argued that the contemporary escalation of mimetic rivalry and accompanying violence in the global economic competition for the remaining natural resources of the planet involved the sacrifice of the earth as the "innocent victim" of contamination by the works of man.[44] The cult of consumerism, sustained by the commercial

---

42. Boenig-Liptsin, "Responses," 267.
43. Girard, *Battling to the End*, 1–27.
44. Girard, *Battling to the End*, 114.

requirement of modern businesses to sell more and more in order to sustain profits and wealth accumulation, is directly responsible for the oblation and scapegoating of the earth, resulting in the destabilization of its climate and diminishing material prospects for future generations.[45] That defenders of the status quo, particularly in the US, tend to scapegoat climate change scientists as the inventors of a false narrative—and legitimize hate, persecution, and violence towards them—further evidences the usefulness of a Girardian analysis to this massive crisis facing humankind.[46]

Girard saw the increasingly likely apocalyptic violent end of humankind as distinct from the mythical kind that Christian fundamentalists believe in, wherein the violence will come from God himself upon his earthly enemies. Rather, the violence will be generated by human beings ourselves, having acquired the means to destroy the whole planet, especially in the volatile post-9/11 climate, with the onset of a globalized conflict between nations and groups that is characterized by an "escalation to extremes."[47] The only cause for hope lies in mimesis of the nonviolence of Christ and his willingness to suffer innocently on behalf of others, thereby renouncing retaliation and the escalation to violent extremes.[48] Jesus' message about the kingdom of God is portrayed as a genuine message of salvation in terms of an eschatological soteriology and a complete break from the violence that binds societies together under the spell of a myth about the need for redemptive violence. Jesus is the Son of God, free of violence from the very beginning and committed to establishing God's radical nonviolence in a culture rooted in violence.[49]

---

45. Northcott, "Girard," 300–301.
46. Northcott, "Girard," 293.
47. Girard, *Battling to the End*, xvi.
48. Girard, *Battling to the End*, 18–19.
49. Palaver, *René Girard's Mimetic Theory*, 209.

Theologians and the Nonviolent Revolution of Jesus

A SOUND THEOLOGICAL BASIS FOR GOSPEL NONVIOLENCE

The thinkers presented in this chapter add considerable weight to the challenge of taking seriously the nonviolence as lived and taught by Jesus as the abiding ethic of living in a violent and broken world. Father John L. McKenzie's work is without equal in terms of explaining the biblical basis for gospel nonviolence in a fully comprehensive manner and how it clashes with the predominant culture of our time. Walter Rauschenbusch emphasized the Christian obligation to social action in the building up of the kingdom of God, which involved a critique of the kind of society that he was living in and how far the church had become implicated in the oppressive structures that characterized it. The revolutionary forces contained within the doctrine of the kingdom as articulated by Rauschenbusch influenced many later thinkers in the twentieth century. Ched Myers's work on radical exegesis informing radical praxis for discipleship can be seen as one such approach to the construction of the "beloved community," as he termed the kingdom of God. The practice of satyagraha, as formulated by Gandhi and heavily influenced by his reading of the Sermon on the Mount, contains the power to break the cycle of violence that runs riot in the world. Christians have only partially realized the power of Jesus' nonviolence in history, but reading afresh the Scriptures, in the way Myers suggests, can inspire a radical return to authentic discipleship. For Girard, the revelation in the Gospels represents humankind's best and only chance of surviving the violent apocalypse that humans themselves have engineered. The scapegoat mechanism that limited human conflict in the past is no longer relevant in these times of potential nuclear holocaust and ecological annihilation. Only adherence to the nonviolence of Jesus can truly save humankind now. It is to the efforts of Pope Francis in returning Jesus' nonviolence to a central role in the practice of Christians in these times of crisis that the next chapter will turn.

4

Towards a Papal Encyclical on Gospel Nonviolence?

THE DIFFERENT STRANDS OF thought of the theologians previously referenced are evident in the way Pope Francis talked on the importance of Christian nonviolence as a central ethic of Christian behavior in the world. This chapter will examine the trajectory of the Catholic Church's return to gospel nonviolence by exploring the various papal pronouncements on war and peace since Vatican II. These have demonstrated a gradual accepting of the centrality of nonviolence to Christian peacemaking in the world, albeit often cloaked in ambiguity over when violent force may sometimes be necessary. I will examine the Vatican-hosted conference "Nonviolence and Just Peace: Contributing to the Catholic Understanding of and Commitment to Nonviolence," which took place in April 2016, as a historic milestone on the return of Catholic teaching towards gospel nonviolence. The work of the participants at the conference contributed directly to Pope Francis's 2017 World Day of Peace message, which pledged the assistance of the church to building peace through creative and active nonviolence in imitation of Jesus. This will be analyzed with a view to the possibility of a papal encyclical on gospel nonviolence that could develop a fuller theoretical and theological elaboration on the ethics of peace-building in the context of a contemporary setting fraught with dangers that threaten the very existence of humankind.

PAPAL PRONOUNCEMENTS ON WAR AND PEACE SINCE VATICAN II

Although just war theory has historically been the most influential framework for Catholic teaching on the use of violence in a political setting, there has always existed a Catholic Christian commitment to peace. Just war theory was intended not to validate certain wars but primarily to restrain them, and as such it was not endorsed officially by the Roman Catholic Church until the *Catechism of the Catholic Church* (1992).[1] Despite being a century like no other in terms of the devastating cost of war to human life, with Christians playing no small role in this, the twentieth century also saw, perhaps paradoxically, a diminution of the just war emphasis in Catholic social teaching, especially after the Second Vatican Council. Although the idea and theory of the just war was never officially repudiated, no pope since the council has approved a war or defended the justice of a war in principle. The emphasis has rather been on abhorring the horror of modern war and promoting the resolution of conflict by peaceful, nonviolent, and democratic means, and on the creation of a just and participatory social, economic, and political order wherein true peace can reside.

Elected as a transitional figure not expected to rock the boat too much, Pope John XXIII in fact brought a revolution to the life of the church in the guise of Vatican II and marked the end of the link between the church and the European Christendom that had come in the wake of the Constantinian shift.[2] His encyclical *Pacem in terris* (1963) built on his earlier encyclical *Mater et magistra* (1961), in which he had emphasized the role of social justice

---

1. Cahill, "Traditional Catholic Thought," 107.
2. Musto, *Catholic Peace Tradition*, 187.

replacing international order as the key to peace.[3] He furthered expounded that the luxury and abundance of the few in the face of the poverty and suffering of the many was an injustice exacerbated by the arms race, which devoted and squandered national wealth into purposes that were destructive and led to the increase of mistrust between peoples.[4] In the nuclear age of warfare, Pope John XXIII was careful in *Pacem in terris* to condemn not only nuclear war but all war as a means of restoring violated rights and in doing so was rejecting one of the bases of the just war theory.[5]

Although Pope John XXIII died between the first and second sessions of the Second Vatican Council, his encyclical had a major influence on the agreed document that arose from it, entitled *Gaudium et spes* (1965). In presenting a pastoral theology of peace, it praised all "who renounce the use of violence in the vindication of their rights."[6] In spite of its legitimating of defensive wars, it severely limited the traditional theory of the just war and called for "an evaluation of war with an entirely new attitude" given the age of total war where scientific weapons cause destruction far exceeding anything like self-defense.[7] The heart of the document, though, lay not in its consideration of war but rather the proclamation of a gospel-inspired active nonviolence capable of encouraging economic, social, and political cooperation among the nations, characterized by a redistribution of the world's wealth[8] and a universal solidarity that would supersede nationalism.[9]

The trajectory towards nonviolence as an authentically Christian and human mandate and practice was continued by successive popes following this extraordinary document that many in the church hoped would end the church's political alliance with

---

3. John XXIII, *Mater et magistra*, §69.
4. John XXIII, *Pacem in terris*, §109.
5. John XXIII, *Pacem in terris*, §127.
6. Second Vatican Council, *Gaudium et spes*, §78.
7. Second Vatican Council, *Gaudium et spes*, §80.
8. Second Vatican Council, *Gaudium et spes*, §88.
9. Second Vatican Council, *Gaudium et spes*, §90.

Towards a Papal Encyclical on Gospel Nonviolence?

secular power and reaffirm its biblical mission to the poor and the oppressed.

Pope Paul VI energetically continued his predecessor's program of reform and work for peace, and in a 1965 address to the UN General Assembly he made an impassioned plea for "an oath that ought to change the future history of the world: never again war, never again war!"[10] In condemning the widening gap between the rich and the poor, he did seem to accept the legitimacy of armed revolution as a means of righting this wrong but qualified this by saying that the evil being fought must not give way to an even greater misery as a result.[11] The only true way to peace, though, was to work for justice, and the church was called to encourage individual Christians to work together at the grassroots level to infuse a Christian spirit into the various social and political structures wherever they live.[12] Most famously, he stated that "the new name for peace is development," although not along the lines of a runaway free-market neoliberalism that leads to an affront to human dignity.[13] Pope John Paul II had a similar view to Pope Paul VI in that he saw violence leading to more injustice and deplored the scale of modern warfare.[14] He did see a role for states to engage in armed action as part of a "humanitarian intervention"[15] to defend populations against the attacks of an unjust aggressor, as had happened in the 1990s in the former Yugoslavia and Rwanda, and he also saw the legitimacy of a nation's right to defense against terrorism.[16] But he famously declared the US Iraq War of 2003 "a defeat for humanity" and urged dialogue and diplomacy instead.[17]

Pope Benedict XVI agreed that the war against Iraq was unjust and, in his writings and speeches, was particularly adamant

10. Paul VI, "Address."
11. Paul VI, *Populorum progressio*, §31.
12. Paul VI, *Populorum progressio*, §81.
13. Paul VI, *Populorum progressio*, §87.
14. Cahill, "Traditional Catholic Thought," 110.
15. John Paul II, "Peace on Earth," §11.
16. John Paul II, "No Peace Without Justice," §5.
17. John Paul II, "Address," §4.

on the centrality of nonviolence at the heart of the gospel message, pondering whether there was any such thing as a "just war" in the present times. He commented during his "Angelus" speech in Saint Peter's Square that "loving the enemy is the nucleus of the 'Christian revolution'" and the "*magna carta*" of Christian nonviolence.[18] He spoke with conviction time and again of the need for Christians to reject violence and find peace through dialogue and solidarity, following the example of Jesus: "In fact it is impossible to interpret Jesus as violent: violence is contrary to the Kingdom of God, it is a tool of the antichrist. Violence is never useful to humanity but dehumanizes it."[19] Like his predecessor, Pope Benedict XVI endorsed humanitarian intervention in accordance with "the principle of the responsibility to protect"[20] but perhaps reflecting skepticism about whether violence could truly end violence he qualified this admission by suggesting it be implemented in "innovative ways."[21]

Pope Francis reaffirmed these same themes as his predecessors upon taking up office at the Vatican in 2013. He was seen as a breath of fresh air by many Catholics and non-Catholics alike for the open, compassionate, and friendly manner that he conducted himself with in public, and he was instrumental as a driving force in the quiet revolution that is seeing the return of gospel nonviolence to the centrality of Catholic teaching. He appealed for international parties in conflict to seek peace by dialogue, most notably when the US and France were threatening a ground invasion of Syria in 2013, joining together with one hundred thousand people at a prayer vigil for peace in Saint Peter's Square and insisting that "violence and war are never the way to peace!"[22] He also appealed to Christians to use nonviolence in seeking reconciliation, stating that "the true strength of the Christian is the power of truth and love, which leads to the renunciation of all violence. Faith and

---

18. Benedict XVI, "Angelus" (2007).
19. Benedict XVI, "Angelus" (2012).
20. Benedict XVI, "Address."
21. Benedict XVI, *Caritas in veritate*, §7.
22. Francis, "Words," §3.

violence are incompatible."²³ In the case of the dilemma of how to deal with the international terrorist organization known as the Islamic State, or ISIS, Francis remarked during an in-flight press conference from Korea to Rome that it was only licit to stop the unjust aggressor, and by this he said he didn't mean dropping bombs. He left it unclear as to what kind of strategies could feasibly be employed against such a very violent and very dangerous opponent but was perhaps signaling that he was going beyond John Paul and Benedict in his view that taking up arms would be justified in a humanitarian intervention or self-defense.²⁴

In writing *Laudato si'*, Pope Francis connected war and ecological destruction that threatens humankind today on a grand scale.²⁵ He was at pains to spell out loud and clear that the very existence of creation is in jeopardy due to the activities of humankind and our adherence to certain social, economic, and political ways of thinking. In doing so Francis provided much analysis on "just how inseparable the bond is between concern for nature, justice for the poor, commitment to society, and interior peace."²⁶ He offered the hope of the gospel to the problems of the world that he described, and he prayed that Christians would "regain the conviction that we need one another, that we have a shared responsibility for others and the world, and that being good and decent are worth it."²⁷ He furthermore decried the hypocrisy of those who talked peace but got rich through the manufacturing of arms, and he rebuked world leaders for failing to find peaceful solutions to global conflicts when he addressed the UN in New York in 2015.²⁸

---

23. Francis, "Angelus."
24. Cahill, "Traditional Catholic Thought," 215–16.
25. Francis, *Laudato si'*, §57.
26. Francis, *Laudato si'*, §10.
27. Francis, *Laudato si'*, §229.
28. Francis, "Address."

THE VATICAN-HOSTED CONFERENCE ON NONVIOLENCE AND JUST PEACE

In the midst of this tragic reality of war and extreme violence, including that being done to the planet, Pope Francis enabled the stage to be set for a fresh appraisal of the challenge of peace and the role of the institutional Catholic Church and wider Catholic community in promoting a path to a just and sustainable peace more in keeping with the consistency of the gospel. From April 11 to April 13, 2016, the Vatican hosted a conference on "Nonviolence and Just Peace: Contributing to the Catholic Understanding of and Commitment to Nonviolence," in which eighty participants from around the world gathered to discuss the Catholic Church's history of and commitment to nonviolence. Perhaps the most striking thing that emerged from the conference was the spread and depth of commitment among Christians throughout the planet engaging in actions inspired by the nonviolence of the gospels, in situations of extreme violence.[29] Each participant was invited to share his or her experiences, leading to deep, serious, and respectful conversations that brought shape and color to the exploration of how the two important concepts of active nonviolence and "just peace" could move the Catholic Church away from the just war tradition.[30]

The rationale for using the term "nonviolence" was explained by US participants Ken Butigan of Pace e Bene and John Dear, SJ. It was seen as a word that not only rejects the use of violence but has a positive and active approach in the use of the power of love and truth in action for justice, peace, and the integrity of creation. It was seen as a clearer way to understanding Jesus' vision than using terms like "love" or "peace" because these have been used by Christians who at the same time have justified support for violence and war. Using the term "nonviolence" makes it more difficult to do this and so can be seen as illuminating the heart of the gospel,

---

29. Dennis, *Choosing Peace*, 7–8.
30. Dennis, *Choosing Peace*, 10.

where Jesus proclaims the reign of God, a new nonviolent order rooted in unconditional love.[31]

Just peace was explained as a Christian school of thought and set of practices for building peace at all stages of acute conflict and the promotion of positive ways to do this. Rooted in the biblical concept of *shalom*, encompassing both a physical and spiritual state of domestic tranquility and neighborliness among nations, the World Council of Churches committed itself to offering direction on the implementation of just peace theology and practice with the publication of its *Just Peace Companion* in 2013.[32]

The participants at the conference were able to grapple with these concepts in the context of the Catholic Church, while daring to imagine what would happen if Catholics from the beginning of their lives were taught to understand and appreciate the power of active nonviolence at the heart of the gospel; the church in turn committed its vast spiritual, intellectual, and financial resources to developing a just peace approach to conflict to prevent atrocities, protect the vulnerable, and safeguard the planet. They were also keen to stress the distinct contribution that the Christian story could make to the ethics of the use of force in the task of peacemaking and in doing so wanted to move away from the tired debate between pacifism and just war theory. The gospel nonviolence they described went way beyond the simple rejection of violence as typified by pacifism. Captured by the example and teaching of Jesus, they endorsed a risk-taking action that confronts violence, using the power of noncooperation, persuasion, selective civil disobedience, and many more strategies of creative nonviolence, which attempts to reach out even to enemies with the power of love capable of melting hearts of stone.[33]

The agreed statement arising from the conference, which was drafted by way of a consensus process, was entitled, "An Appeal to the Catholic Church to Re-Commit to the Centrality of Gospel Nonviolence." In it, they recognized the encouraging words of Pope

---

31. Dennis, *Choosing Peace*, 11.
32. Berger, "Catholic Just Peace Practice," 169.
33. Dennis, *Choosing Peace*, 218–19.

Francis to the conference in which he stated that the revitalization of the tools of active nonviolence would be a much-needed and positive contribution. It also set out the rationale for appealing to the church to invest "far greater human and financial resources in promoting a spirituality and practice of active nonviolence and in forming and training our Catholic communities in effective nonviolent practices."[34] More specific requests were that the just war theory no longer be used or taught and that Pope Francis would share with the world an encyclical on nonviolence and just peace, which would aid those nonviolent activists whose work for peace and justice in challenging unjust world powers was putting their lives at risk. A sincere hope was expressed that further collaboration would happen between the organizers and participants of the conference, the Holy See, and the global church in advancing gospel nonviolence.[35]

WORLD DAY OF PEACE MESSAGE, 2017: "NONVIOLENCE: A STYLE OF POLITICS FOR PEACE"

Although the Pontifical Council for Justice and Peace staff members participated actively in many parts of the conference proceedings, the final document was a message to the Vatican and was not signed or endorsed by the Pontifical Council.[36] However, Pope Francis's World Day of Peace message in 2017 was certainly a sign that this hope for furthering the advancement of gospel nonviolence was being realized with the leadership of the Catholic Church. Entitled "Nonviolence: A Style of Politics for Peace," his message referenced the statements of previous popes, extolling a hope for peace founded upon truth, justice, freedom, and love, and it reflected on making active nonviolence the way of life not just for Christians but a real option for those involved in politics.[37] He

34. Dennis, *Choosing Peace*, 23.
35. Dennis, *Choosing Peace*, 25–26.
36. Dennis, *Choosing Peace*, 202.
37. Francis, "Nonviolence," §1.

lamented the vast amount of resources dedicated to military ends away from the everyday needs of people most in need, who suffer most in the horrifying "world war fought piecemeal."[38] He affirmed that the nonviolent teachings of Jesus were to be embraced by those wishing to be true followers and referenced examples from history of Christians and people of other faiths in waging nonviolent struggles that have produced impressive results in the real world as a way of emphasizing that nonviolence entails anything but a lack of involvement and passivity.[39] Emphatically reaffirming that the name of God cannot be used to justify violence, he pledged the "assistance of the Church in every effort to build peace through active and creative nonviolence."[40]

Responses to the publication of Pope Francis's message from participants in the conference were overwhelmingly positive. Terrence Rynne saw it as a major breakthrough and a clear sign of the Catholic Church's return to the sources of sacred Scripture and the traditions of the early church.[41] He believed that the Pope had laid out in no uncertain terms that nonviolent direct action is a substitute for war. In much the same way as other institutions of violence, like slavery, had been taken as a given by society and were replaced by a new consciousness, war in time would be replaced by a consciousness that nonviolence is not only preferable to the destruction of war but that it also works.[42] Rynne believed that Pope Francis should have fully developed how nonviolent direct action operated by writing an encyclical that could delve more deeply into the historical successes of nonviolence that he briefly referenced in his peace message. However, what he had produced in his message had given nonviolence a pride of place and was a continuation of progressively giving more space to the subject by popes since Vatican II.[43]

38. Francis, "Nonviolence," §2.
39. Francis, "Nonviolence," §§3, 4.
40. Francis, "Nonviolence," §6.
41. Rynne, "Responses," 232.
42. Rynne, "Responses," 233.
43. Rynne, "Responses," 237.

For moral theologian and conference participant Gerald Schlabach, Pope Francis's World Day of Peace message employed a good deal of savvy Vatican rhetoric in order to balance considerations and forge consensus on an issue of a complex global nature. He saw it alluding to the just war theory in terms of "the church's continuing efforts to limit the use of force by the application of moral norms."[44] By not calling this the "just war" theory by name, Pope Francis was leaving it neither rejected nor defended. Far from validating its continued use, Schlabach saw Pope Francis as making a bold claim that the Sermon on the Mount should be the "manual" for peacemaking, not just for saintly Christians but for all those involved in the public realm, hence the titling of his peace message a "style of *politics* for peace."[45] Schlabach believed that Catholic peace-builders should have been grateful for the pope's message as a sure sign that the Vatican was listening but at the same time shouldn't expect too much too soon, even in a possible encyclical on gospel nonviolence. He pointed out that it was highly unrealistic to expect Pope Francis to have taken down the just war theory in one fell swoop, as to do so would be to say that the great Christian authorities and theologians of the past got it wrong. Others might argue that it would be possible to take it down as a theory due to its inappropriateness for the modern age of total war. Nevertheless, he predicted that the just war theory would be damned with faint praise in finessed language or killed with a thousand cuts, whereupon it was up to Catholic peace-builders to amplify the positive signals for active nonviolence emanating from official papal statements like Francis's World Day of Peace message.[46]

Pope Francis continued the advancement of Gospel nonviolence throughout the rest of his papacy, culminating in his endorsement of the 2024 inauguration of the Pax Christi International Catholic Institute for Nonviolence, a movement consisting of 120 organizations from all around the world dedicated to promoting

---

44. Schlabach, "Responses," 238.
45. Schlabach, "Responses," 239.
46. Schlabach, "Responses," 240.

nonviolence as a central teaching of the Catholic Church and embarking on the mission of making research, resources, and experiences in nonviolence more accessible both for church leaders and global institutions.[47] He also marked the sixtieth anniversary of the declaration of Saint Pope John XXIII's encyclical *Pacem in terris* by pleading for the world to pray for a "nonviolent culture."[48] In his April 2023 prayer intention sent out on his worldwide prayer network to around three hundred thousand people, Francis prayed, "Let us make nonviolence a guide for our actions both in daily life and in international relations. And let us pray for a more widespread culture of nonviolence that will progress when countries and citizens alike resort less and less to the use of arms."[49]

Having decried that the world was experiencing "a third world war fought piecemeal,"[50] a global culture of violence including permanent war, growing poverty, threats to civil liberties, ecological devastation, the enduring terror of nuclear weapons, and the scourge of the structural violence of racism, sexism, and economic injustice and other forms of systemic injustice, Pope Francis advocated time and again that the answer to this violence was not more violence but rather active nonviolence that combines the rejection of violence with the power of love and reconciliation in action. He recognized that such a shift in approach required nothing more than a profound *metanoia* and he implored Christians to look anew at the example and teachings of Jesus to inform their lives as followers of Christ:

> We must necessarily find the answers to these questions in the Gospel: in Jesus, who calls us to be merciful and never violent, to be perfect as the Father is perfect, and not be conformed to the world. . . . Christ is our peace. By his incarnation, death, and resurrection for all, he has torn down the walls of enmity and division between people . . . but we also need to experience conversion,

---

47. Merlo, "Cardinal McElroy."
48. Watkins, "Pope's April Prayer Intention."
49. Watkins, "Pope's April Prayer Intention."
50. Francis, *Against War*, 45.

and to recognize that armed conquest, expansionism and imperialism have nothing to do with the Kingdom that Jesus proclaimed.[51]

MOVING BEYOND THE JUST WAR VS. PACIFISM DEBATE

It seems eminently clear that the Catholic Church, inspired as it was by the charismatic leadership of Pope Francis, is returning gospel nonviolence back to a central role in its approach to issues of war and peace, even if it still has a bit to go. While it, like most Christian churches, maintains a just war position in regard to conflict, the more that is revealed about the bloody cost of it in terms of human life and the grave environmental crisis that it is linked to, the less space is given to any talk of justified war. Even many theologians who are open to the possibility of a just war are reluctant to admit that governments should have a carte blanche when it comes to the preparations for and actual conduct of war. For example, former Archbishop of Canterbury Rowan Williams, who is supportive in principle of a just war theory when its principles are rigorously applied, in a scholarly debate with George Weigel cautioned the latter in his use of just war theory to recognize that it has at its heart a presumption against violence in the tradition. Therefore any preemptive wars in the interests of national security by the US or any other country cannot be justified per se, based on a serious consideration of the just war theory's constraints on using violent coercion.[52] On a practical level, having a presumption-against-war framework in relation to the just war theory was seen by renowned Mennonite biblical scholar John Yoder as having the potential to save more lives than any outright condemnation of violence as contrary to the will of God.[53]

---

51. Lubov, "Pope: Christian Reconciliation."
52. Williams and Weigel, "War and Statecraft," 387–90.
53. Yoder, "Just War and Nonviolence," 85–87.

Rowan Williams's critique of Western society's pathology of fear, which gives rise to the kinds of madness that threaten the very survival of humankind like "mutually assured destruction," also serves to bolster the arguments for applying gospel nonviolence as a central ethic for Christian living.[54] Herbert McCabe, another theologian of the recent past, raged against the dominant global economic system of capitalism and its relationship to the interlocking complexity of evil that grips humankind in the world.[55] These theologians illustrate there is great scope to move beyond the polarizing "just war vs. pacifism" paradigm of theological debate and instead work towards Christian unity based on preventing war in the first place by critiquing what needs to be done in creating more just and humane social conditions through practices of just peacemaking.[56] Gerald Schlabach suggests that just war teaching can be seen as a "traditional righteousness" in the mold of Glen Stassen's exegesis on the Sermon on the Mount as a series of triads. As such, the "transforming initiatives," as offered by theologians on gospel nonviolence, can be used in dialogue with those followers of Christ who advocate just war as a way out of the "vicious cycle" that this "traditional righteousness" has produced.[57]

THE URGENCY OF PROCLAIMING GOSPEL NONVIOLENCE IN A BROKEN WORLD

That Pope Francis advocated so consistently for Christians to embrace Jesus' teachings on nonviolence in their lives is very encouraging for proponents of gospel nonviolence. For those suffering at the coalface of conflict, the questions of nonviolence and just war are far from theoretical. Jesuit priest Francis De Roux spoke at the April 2016 conference on his desire to see the church abandon the just war perspective due to the scandalous harm it had brought

---

54. Williams, *Truce of God*, 10–12.
55. McCabe, *God Still Matters*, 168–69.
56. Schlabach, "'Confessional' Nonviolence," 140.
57. Schlabach, "Confessional' Nonviolence," 133–34.

to his country of Colombia. He pointed out that priests and nuns had joined the National Liberation Army in the 1960s and 1970s because of the just war theory, not because of reading liberation theology. The Colombian state army too is trapped in a just war paradigm and has had a long association with Catholic symbolism, with many military bases containing shrines to the Virgin Mary—the same Virgin Mary that paramilitaries often pray to before going off to kill their enemies. The net result for Colombia has been a living hell for its people according to De Roux.[58]

As a Latin American pope who lived through his country's own period of hell during the "dirty war" of the dictatorship years in Argentina, Pope Francis would not have been unsympathetic to such witness. He went through his own period of reflection on the horror of torture and killing in the wake of Jesuits being taken by the military junta while he was the leader of the Jesuit order. They were only but a few of the many thousands imprisoned, tortured, killed, and disappeared by a regime that enjoyed the support and blessing of many senior figures in the Catholic Church in Argentina. Thus, his papacy was characterized by empathy for people suffering in the world, particularly as a result of sinful human structures and systems. The return of gospel nonviolence to a central place in the church's teaching on issues of war and peace has been gathering pace since the Second Vatican Council, and Pope Francis made huge strides in giving it space to be debated and taken seriously as a central way of building the kingdom of God. As an institution whose reach is global, the Roman Catholic Church can lead the way in amplifying gospel nonviolence by promoting its teaching in Catholic churches, seminaries, schools, and universities throughout the world, particularly in this age of instant and mass communication. The question of course is whether the church as a whole is ready for this much-needed renewal. Again, the words of Pope Francis give counsel on what needs to be done.

> As Jesus "shook" the doctors of the law to break them free of their rigidity, now also the Church is "shaken" by the Spirit in order to lay aside comforts and attachments.

58. De Roux, "The Church," 204.

We should not be afraid of renewal. The Church always needs renewal—*Ecclesia semper renovanda*. She does not renew herself on her own whim, but rather does so "firm in the faith, stable and steadfast, not shifting from the hope of the gospel" (Col 1:23). Renewal entails sacrifice and courage, not so that we can consider ourselves superior or flawless, but rather to respond better to the Lord's call. The Lord of the Sabbath, the reason for our commandments and prescriptions, invites us to reflect on regulations when our following him is at stake; when his open wounds and his cries of hunger and thirst for justice call out to us and demand new responses.[59]

Although spoken in Colombia, these words echoed a challenge for the entire church to better respond to the Lord's call. It is the potential of the Irish Church to renew itself to the demands of gospel nonviolence that will now be examined in the rest of the book.

---

59. Francis, "Christian Life."

5

Gospel Nonviolence and the Renewal of the Irish Church

THE IRISH CATHOLIC CHURCH is at once experiencing a time of steep decline in influence and relevance in Ireland and at the same time going through somewhat of a renewal. This renewal has coincided with the path of synodality initiated by Pope Francis and continued by his successor Pope Leo XIV towards a church that listens to each other and the Holy Spirit in order to discern and proclaim the gospel. It is the opportune time for the Irish Church to take inspiration from the prophetic witness to gospel nonviolence that characterized the papacy of Pope Francis and make this the cornerstone of a renewed church faithful in Ireland. The unique history of the Irish Church makes it well placed to become a beacon for the rest of the Christian churches in the world to teach and be the example of Jesus' radical command to live out active nonviolence in imitation of the God of love.

Gospel Nonviolence and the Renewal of the Irish Church

THE IRISH CHURCH AND A HISTORY OF VIOLENT IMPERIALISM

The task of building consciousness around gospel nonviolence among church authorities and laity alike in Ireland is not a small one. The Irish Church, like so many other churches in the world, has had a long and difficult relationship with the subject of violence throughout its history. At various times in its history, church authorities have sided simultaneously with the oppressor and the oppressed during the long period of struggle for independence from British rule and indeed in different circumstances after the Treaty of 1921, which saw Ireland partitioned and the Catholic Church rise to political prominence in the new Irish Free State. It has also been at the forefront of attempts at conflict resolution throughout Irish history, none more so than the recent peace process to end the conflict that ravaged the northern part of Ireland and beyond for over thirty years. The net result of this for ordinary Catholics of course is a completely ambiguous message when it comes to the justified use of violence. This is no surprise given the Constantinian shift and the effective sidelining of gospel nonviolence as a central pillar of Christian witness in the world.

Similar to other countries' experience of settler-colonial imperialism by so-called "Christian" nations, Ireland has felt the effects of the just war theory, employed by both the oppressor and the oppressed. The invasion of Ireland by the Normans in 1171, led by King Henry II of England, was given ecclesiastical sanction by Pope Adrian IV, the only English pope in history. This papal approval came in the form of a papal bull known as *Laudabiliter*, issued around 1155.[1] The justification given was that the Irish needed religious correction and civil governance, a theme common in colonial theology, found especially with the Spanish and Portuguese conquests of the Americas. The campaign of Cromwell in the middle of the 1600s was probably the starkest example of this theological justification for killing for righteousness' sake. Inspired by religious zeal, the "divine justice" he unleashed on what

---

1. Nicholls, *Gaelic and Gaelicised Ireland*, 78–79.

he considered an idolatrous Catholic population left thousands of men, women, and children dead and a legacy of lasting bitterness towards English rule in the centuries to come.

Against this brutal oppression, the robbery of their lands in the plantations, and the outlawing of the Catholic faith with the penal laws, many in Ireland, quite understandably, decided to respond with violence of their own against their overlords and thus fueled the spiral of violence that marked the centuries that followed. Many were inspired by the secular influences they saw in first the American and then the French revolutions, but given the deeply ingrained religious traditions in Ireland, it was only natural that Christian faith would be intertwined with the violent struggles to rid Ireland of its colonial oppressor.

The Catholic mysticism, spirituality, and religious symbolism exuded in the writings of some of the leaders of the 1916 Rising before their executions are probably the clearest example of how a deeply held Christian faith became embedded with the justification for armed rebellion. Patrick Pearse's idea of a blood sacrifice mirrored the crucifixion narrative of the nation being redeemed by the blood of its martyrs. He linked the deaths of himself and other Irish rebels to the sacrifice of Christ; like the resurrection that followed, the Irish nation would rise again also.[2] While church authorities typically condemned or lauded those who fought and died for Irish freedom, the absence of any teaching on the part of the Catholic Church on the powerful alternative of active nonviolence as taught and lived by Jesus meant that those who engaged in violent combat did so with their consciences fully clear. If the Irishmen going off to kill and die in World War I were being lauded and deemed fit for Holy Communion before slaughtering their fellow man, then it did not take a huge leap of the imagination to believe that engaging in armed conflict against one of the world's most notorious and oppressive colonial powers should also be seen as right and just by the church faithful.

During the Troubles these trends continued, and many people of the Christian faith, Catholic and Protestant alike, engaged in

2. Pearse, "Coming Revolution," 367–71.

acts of violence with clear consciences, believing that their actions were fully justified, while appeals from different church figures for an end to armed means went unheeded, littered as they were with glaring inconsistencies. For a lot of IRA men of Catholic faith and others who joined armed republican groups, any calls for an abandonment of armed struggle from church leaders were laden with a lack of moral authority. This was based on a rudimentary understanding of the just war theory and the historic failure of the church to consistently condemn all expressions of violence as being contrary to the building of the kingdom of God. The peaceful, nonviolent means of the civil rights movement had been tried and ultimately failed to bring about either a cessation of the state repression that was being sharply felt at that time or indeed the united Ireland that so many Catholics in the north longed for as a legitimate political desire. The next logical step after all peaceful means had been exhausted was armed defense, one of the tenets of the just war theory. Indeed, there were priests and other religious figures who encouraged and actively helped in the development of this armed defense, inspired no doubt by the presence of the official church at commemorations for 1916 and other violent events in Irish history, which gave these acts of resistance church blessing. Any church leaders who tried to distinguish between the taking up of arms in the past and the violent means for liberation now being taken were easily dismissed by republicans as hypocrites and as lacking a proper understanding of Irish history.

On the loyalist and British side, "For God and Ulster" was a common slogan used to sanctify the people who were violently defending the British crown from its traditional heathen enemies. For a people who had lived in the northern part of Ireland for nearly four centuries, their cherished Protestant faith marked them apart from their Catholic neighbors, whom they viewed with a deep mistrust. Despite the violent conquest that enabled their arrival to Ireland, they viewed their presence on this island as pleasing to the just and righteous God who had blessed them as a holy people within the glorious British Empire. Never a second's thought would have been given that the violence perpetrated by this empire throughout its long and bloody existence was anything other than ordained by God. For all the differences among the various shades of Christianity that had existed since the massive schism of the church during the Reformation, there was one point of agreement they all shared, and that was the divine righteousness of their own violence, wholly at odds with the revelation of the nonviolent God through his Son Jesus Christ.

There were of course people within the Christian churches who went to great lengths to promote peace and dialogue during the era of the conflict in the north of Ireland who relied courageously on using nonviolent means, sometimes at great cost to themselves and their reputations. Two of the most notable examples were Father Denis Faul and Father Raymond Murray, who exposed the crimes of torture and abuse of political prisoners in the notorious Maze and Armagh prisons. Their documentation of these grave human rights abuses brought to light the systematic nature of the use of torture in British jails and embarrassed the British state, which preferred to keep such policies hidden from public view. This simple act of gathering firsthand testimony from the victims of such abuses and publishing them in leaflets and pamphlets for dissemination among the general public was characteristic of the kinds of active nonviolence that Jesus called his followers to practice. The risks in doing so at that time were great but these priests embraced any suffering that came their way as the price to be paid for following Jesus' way of nonviolent love of friends and enemies.

The hunger strikes by republican prisoners in the Maze prison in 1981, resulting in the deaths of ten men, also took on the character of nonviolent redemptive suffering. Regardless of why these men were in prison, they decided to hunger and thirst against a brutal prison regime that was meant to crush their human spirit. In this battle of wills, the prisoners wished to be treated as political prisoners and not as criminals as the British government was characterizing them. The spiral of violence had brought them to this place, and as the British government policy of criminalization played out, it was decided that a hunger strike, reminiscent of the old Irish Brehon laws and infused with a Christian theological grounding in the Beatitudes, would be embarked upon to resist the horrendous, inhuman conditions that they were living in. While Father Denis Faul opposed the hunger strike, in his conversations with the republican prisoner Bobby Sands, who was leading the fast and would ultimately go on to die first, Sands quoted John 15:13—"Greater love has no man than this, that a man lay down his life for his friends"—to justify the protest as an act of self-sacrificial love in the same vein as Jesus' sacrifice on the cross. Father Faul had no argument to counter this.[3]

Other members of the clergy, both Catholic and Protestant, engaged in strenuous efforts to promote back-channel dialogue between the warring sides to reach a cessation of violence and ultimately some kind of a political solution. There was never, however, a theology of nonviolence coming from church authorities that underpinned these efforts.

THE GOSPEL NONVIOLENCE OF THE PEACE PEOPLE

One of the rare examples of someone who embodied and worked for peace during the Troubles from a position of gospel nonviolence was Mairead Corrigan Maguire. She founded the Peace People in 1976 along with Betty Williams and Ciarán McKeown after a series of tragic events related to the conflict and in particular the deaths of her niece Johanne (aged eight and a half) and her two nephews, John (aged two-and-a-half) and Andrew (six weeks old). They died when a British army patrol shot and killed a nineteen-year-old IRA volunteer, Danny Lennon; the car driven by him crashed onto the footpath, killing the children and seriously injuring their mother, Anne, who was Mairead's sister. Within weeks of this event in August 1976, tens of thousands of people across the north of Ireland took to the streets demanding an end to the violence.[4] On the back of this the Peace People com-

---

3. Taylor, "Behind the Mask."
4. Maguire, *Vision of Peace*, 3.

mitted themselves to working nonviolently for reconciliation and justice in the north of Ireland but also, importantly, connecting with people and movements working nonviolently for change in other parts of the world. There was a real optimism in the air that this people-powered grassroots movement would bear fruit and that the conflict would cease for talks to begin.[5] In the end, tensions within the movement on where the focus should lie and whether some issues were too political caused the Peace People to split in 1980, and the initial sense of optimism that it had as a force for a real change dissipated.[6]

Perhaps part of the problem the movement had faced was that the roots for understanding and embodying nonviolent peacemaking, as consistent with the commands of Jesus in the Gospels, were too shallow as a result of the failure of the broad Christian church to effectively teach and live out gospel nonviolence as one of its core elements of existence. Mairead's vision of nonviolence was not well received at a time when violence and vengeance filled the hearts of many. "Nonviolence" was an unpopular word, associated with weakness and naivety and thus easily dismissed, ridiculed, and ignored.[7]

Despite Mairead going to great lengths to ground her devotion to active nonviolence in the Christian faith and drawing parallels with the work of others throughout the world involved in using active nonviolence to challenge injustice and oppression, there was a strongly held false perception, especially among republicans, that while she criticized IRA violence, she was soft on the violence perpetrated by virtue of the British military occupation of Ireland. It was likened to the stance taken by Pope John Paul II on his papal visit to Ireland where he issued a strong condemnation of the use of violence but did not condemn the British army directly.[8] Given the neutrality of Vatican diplomacy he would not have risked doing such a thing in any case, but there was no call

5. Maguire, *Vision of Peace*, 6–7.
6. Maguire, *Vision of Peace*, 8.
7. Maguire, *Vision of Peace*, xviii.
8. John Paul II, "Holy Mass in Drogheda."

to address the injustices that gave rise to the conflict with active nonviolence. The IRA rejected his call as naïve, one-sided, and failing to address the root causes of the conflict, namely, British rule in the north of Ireland. Without an explicit reference to the revolutionary practice of gospel nonviolence, it was always going to be so that people would find alternative means to address injustice, even if it meant violence, and given the ambiguous messaging from church authorities on this, any moral appeal to desist from violent means would always be problematic.

The Peace People, led by Mairead Corrigan Maguire in the years following the split, knew this well and appealed to the Catholic Church to develop a theology of nonviolence grounded in the teaching and life of Jesus.[9] She attended the three-day global summit on nonviolence in 2016, cohosted in Rome by the Pontifical Council for Justice and Peace and Pax Christi; and together with bishops, theologians, and laypeople, she called on Pope Francis to issue an encyclical on nonviolence and just peace, urging the church to reject the just war theory and instead uphold nonviolent transformation. She believed that this could make an enormous contribution to the cause of peace in Ireland and also in the world.[10]

THE URGENT CHALLENGE OF GOSPEL NONVIOLENCE

The challenge for the Irish Church is the same challenge that faces the rest of the church worldwide, and that is to teach what Jesus taught as regards nonviolent love of friends and enemies. The lack of a prophetic voice on peace and justice grounded in the radical demands of gospel nonviolence coming from the church in Ireland needs to be urgently addressed. Many lives could have been saved from the consequences of violence throughout Irish history if gospel nonviolence had been taught and embodied by the leadership of the church. Today, the conflict in Ireland may have quietened

---

9. Maguire, *Vision of Peace*, 110.
10. Maguire, *Vision of Peace*, 111.

but other conflicts are raging in other parts of the world that require the prophetic critique of gospel nonviolence to inspire nonviolent solutions. Too often the dominant narrative being heard in Ireland is coming from a media that uncritically supports war and war-making as part of the human fabric of society. The military industrial complex has its lobbyists busy working to stoke up fears of Ireland being vulnerable to attack from the likes of Russia, suggesting that the only "mature" response is to ready ourselves with massive investment in our army and weaponry. This is something Christians need to challenge in the spirit of the nonviolent Jesus.

Jesus wept over Jerusalem, crying out, "If you, even you, had known on this day the things that make for peace! But now they are hidden from your eyes" (Luke 19:41–42). The Irish Church is very careful with its language when it comments of matters of war and peace but very often lacks the courageous prophetic edge that Jesus taught his followers to imitate in a spirit of nonviolent love. Two examples from the conflicts that dominate much of the current discourse around war and peace will illustrate the point being made here.

IRELAND AND THE UKRAINE WAR

Since its partial independence from Britain, Ireland has maintained a path of military neutrality as the wars have raged in the world, a stance that receives widespread public support. However, given the outbreak of the first full-scale war on European soil since World War II, there have been vigorous attempts by many in the ruling political classes, backed by media commentators, for Ireland to abandon its military neutrality and to demonstrate its "maturity" as a modern nation.

When Queen Elizabeth visited Ireland in 2011, there was a sense generated of the chapter closing on Ireland's violent history with its colonial oppressor, even though the north of Ireland remained under British jurisdiction. There was talk of a "shared" history, and both Irish men fighting for independence and British forces fighting to maintain the empire were being commemorated in state-led ceremonies in the interest of promoting reconciliation between historical enemies. The week after the queen of England left, the president of the US, Barack Obama, arrived in Ireland to a raucous welcome. A new chapter, brewing for quite some time, was being officially celebrated in Ireland, that of the political alliance with the US empire and all that came with it. Ireland, now mature, would stand with the US as a global partner and build on its special relationship forged through centuries of emigration. The old tendencies to identify Ireland as a champion of resistance to imperialism now belonged to history. A foreign policy uncritical of US militarism was far more pragmatic and beneficial for economic growth. Added to this was Ireland's growing stature as a member of the US' allies in Europe, the EU. Accordingly, as part of an increasingly militarized European Union, Ireland had the chance to show off its maturity as a nation by growing its military budget, citing the threats to world peace coming primarily from Russia. The broad mainstream media have played their part, too, in promoting the logic of war preparations in a dangerous world while at the same time dismissing alternative anti-war views as naïve and childish.

At the height of this Ukraine-Russia War, RTÉ Prime Time ran a feature piece on a young man from Rathmines in Dublin, born to Ukrainian parents, who had gone off to fight with the Ukrainian military. In it he described his motivations for joining the war effort and what life was like on the front lines. It was only a few weeks later, at the end of August 2024, that the news came through that this twenty-year-old man had been declared missing and presumed dead.[11] He is one of hundreds of thousands of casualties in a conflict that has its roots well beyond 2022, but which spiraled into full-scale warfare with the Russian invasion of Ukraine in that year. Other Irishmen have also been among the casualties, and their motivations for fighting were no doubt as sincere as their fellow volunteers who were outraged by the injustice of the Russian invasion and all the horrors that followed from this. As with all wars, though, propaganda has obscured the truth of what

11. Prime Time Team, "Dubliner Missing."

led to the conflict breaking out and what indeed has been the reality of the conflict on the ground. The question to be asked is whether these deaths could have been avoided by a Christian response that condemned the use and threat of violence coming from all sides and instead promoted a nonviolent solution to the conflict.

RTÉ themselves were very quick and willing to paint the conflict in no uncertain terms as good vs. evil. The Russian bad guys started the war unjustly and had to be stopped by all means necessary. RTÉ radio drive-time programs that reported on the early stages of the conflict were filled with Ukrainian voices appealing for more and more military aid to fight the Russians, who were depicted as monsters incapable of engaging in dialogue to put an end to the slaughter. The Irish government was coming under pressure from various moral crusaders to end Ireland's policy of military neutrality, which was characterized as immature and cowardly. Voices condemning the escalation into full-scale war and calling for a peaceful resolution to the conflict were ridiculed, and many were labeled as Russian puppets. The narrative quickly took hold in Ireland that there was no alternative to a military victory for the Ukrainians over the despotic Russians, and anyone deviating from that script had better be ready for a very public backlash.

The Irish Catholic Church, following the lead taken by Pope Francis, has been consistently vocal in its response to the war in Ukraine, emphasizing the principles of peace, justice, and humanitarian aid. Archbishop of Dublin Dermot Farrell rightly condemned Russia's invasion as a "brutal, cynical violation of international law and human dignity."[12] While it called for an end to the killing and for peaceful dialogue to take place, no condemnations were made of the role NATO leaders had played in the conflict, and no efforts were made to promote understanding of the context in which the brutal Russia invasion had taken place.

It can be argued that it is not the job of the church to educate people on the nuances of the current geopolitical situation in the world, but employing language that recognizes more than one side to the story goes a long way towards enabling a nonviolent

12. Farrell, "My Heart."

solution to the conflict to be found. While the context to the Russian invasion of Ukraine is quite complex, the armed conflict that broke out in 2014 following the ousting of democratically elected and Moscow-backed President Yanukovych had resulted in the deaths of thousands, especially ethnic Russians in Eastern Ukraine. The potential expansion of NATO into Ukraine, one step closer to Russia's borders, was a red line for Russia, but Western powers ignored their concerns and goaded Russia into a response. When the Russian invasion came, the Western powers duly threw a few weapons at the Ukrainians and wished them all the best in their fight. While they refrained from direct military intervention to avoid a wider war, they showed no hesitation in fueling the conflict from a distance, content to see young Ukrainians die on the battlefield as their investments in the arms industry grew ever more profitable. None of these facts give any moral justification to the Russian military invasion and the horrific slaughter that has happened since. It is sufficient to say that church criticism of Russia and only Russia as the guilty protagonist in this war betrays the reality of Western governments' complicity in the escalation of the situation and, even more dangerously, led to a justification of the pouring in of weapons to Ukraine that has fueled the resistance of their country but left thousands of young people dead.

It also led to situations like what occurred outside Donnycarney Church on a Sunday afternoon in 2023, as a van pulled up after the noon mass inscribed with "military.ie" on the side of it. Only the week before, a collection had been taken up at all the weekend masses to provide logistical support for those involved in the terrifying situation in Ukraine. As the van was unloaded by a handful of volunteers, it was clear that the boxes they were carrying into the church building were full of the military grade equipment that would have been of great necessity in the battlefields to keep the soldiers fighting there warm and prepared for the travails that awaited them as the war raged on. Inside the church that morning, prayers were said for peace, while outside the church that morning, preparations were being made for the war effort.

By not calling out all sides for their addiction to military means, the church was maintaining a long tradition of politically aligning itself with the West and in doing so contributing to the enmity towards Russia and a more polarized world. It is in the interests of the Western governments, especially those in NATO, to have Russia held up to the world as an enemy and thus justify the massive investments in the military industrial complex. The same need for an external enemy of course applies to Russia and any country whose massive military budget needs justifying. It is, however, the responsibility of the church in building up the kingdom of God not to align itself politically with any group of nations in the world, but to call for disarmament and active nonviolence as the response to conflicts that arise among and within nations. The fact that the majority of those doing the fighting are from nations where Christianity is the main religion illustrates the failures associated with not having a theology of gospel nonviolence taught and lived out among people in the different nations where Christians make up the majority.

IRELAND AND THE GENOCIDE IN GAZA

When Hamas attacked Israel on October 7, 2023, the world's media was quick to express shock at such violence and frame the response that followed from Israel in terms of legitimate self-defense against terrorism. Very quickly it became apparent, though, that this "legitimate" response was callously targeting whole swathes of Gazan cities and towns, resulting in the killings of thousands of civilians and the kinds of suffering, especially of children, that the world thought they had left consigned to history. In stark contrast to its reporting on the Ukraine war, the Irish media was careful to report on the daily slaughter inflicted by Israeli forces in what it considered a "balanced" way. Whereas Russia was the bad guy and Ukraine the victim, in this conflict there was no such moralizing on the events taking place, apart from the condemnation of Hamas, who was seen to have "started" the "war." Israeli military statements blaming Hamas for using civilians as human shields were reported on as plausible explanations for the high casualty rate among the Gazan civilian population. Hamas was painted as the original cause for the suffering taking place, and Israel was only guilty of perhaps being overzealous in their attempts to wipe out the terrorist threat to their existence. Any criticism of Israel, though, would lead to accusations of anti-Semitism, and so the media were largely muted in their reporting of the scale of the suffering, and the governments of the Western world were careful not to say anything beyond urging restraint as Israel went about their genocide of the Palestinian people.

Over time, as the evidence piled up of the sheer volume of atrocities being committed by Israeli forces, the Irish government and others began to more vociferously criticize the Israeli government's military policy in Gaza. Once the predictable but ridiculous assertions of anti-Semitism were faced down, the Irish government continued to call for a ceasefire and humanitarian aid to help the Gazans living through hell on earth. The Irish Catholic Bishop's Conference seemed to echo the stance of the Irish government by condemning the "daily horror of killing, wounding and destruction," urging both the Israeli government and Hamas to respect basic human and international standards, including unhindered access to food, water, and safety for civilians.[13] They called for "courageous world leadership to stop the Israel/Hamas war" and urged the cutting off of arms supplies for what they termed Israel's "genocidal actions."[14]

On the face of it, beyond making public statements using strong and deliberate language to call for a ceasefire and humanitarian aid, the Irish government and the Irish Church couldn't have been accused of not trying to help alleviate the dreadful suffering of the Palestinian people. This, however, masks the fact that there is always much more that could have been done. In the case of the Irish government, the stranglehold of realpolitik meant that they continued to engage in trade with Israel, with recent data showing that Ireland had emerged as Israel's second-largest export

13. Irish Catholic Bishops' Conference, "Let Us All."
14. Irish Catholic Bishops' Conference, "Irish Bishops Call."

destination for goods, only behind the US.[15] In addition, the Irish Central Bank continued to facilitate the sale of Israeli bonds that help to fund the devastation in Gaza and the occupied West Bank, with the Irish government refusing to intervene on the matter.[16]

While peace activists naturally react with fury to the stubborn refusal of the Irish government to back up their words with real actions that could make a bigger impact and inspire action from other states, the reality of the capitalist system and the need to curry favor with big multinational corporations to keep the economy roaring means that governments are never likely to strive too far from limited protest to the injustices of the world. The Christian church on the other hand, given the mandate from Jesus to be a light in the darkness of a suffering humanity, has no such excuse to be timid on what needs to change for a just and peaceful social order to emerge on earth. It demands individual and collective actions from Christians all over the world to halt the war machine that is being unleashed with brutal openness upon the people of Gaza. Yet, Christians in their millions continue daily to do jobs that enable each cog of this machine to function with incredible efficiency. Church leaders need to speak louder about what it takes to stop the slaughter and work on solutions that lead to conflict resolution. Among other potential actions, they could call for Christians to refuse to work in jobs that enable the ferocity of the military industrial complex to flourish in the world, promote a boycott of voting for politicians who continually vote for armed solutions to the world's problems, and encourage soldiers to look into their conscience and consider conscientious objection to participating in wars that tear human lives asunder. This, the church can only do with any moral authority by having the principles of gospel nonviolence as the basis of their public pronouncements on matters of war and peace.

---

15. Burke-Kennedy, "Despite the Politics."
16. Brennan, "Central Bank."

BREAKING FROM THE DOMINATION SYSTEM OF THE EMPIRE

The church at one and the same time needs to engage in an honest reflection about its historic violent alliance with the kingdoms of the world and build on the efforts already happening to flood the world with the good news of God's salvific nonviolent love of friends and enemies. Two prominent theologians that have already contributed to a critique of Christian behavior in the world are Herbert McCabe and Rowan Williams. Herbert McCabe, in his book *God Still Matters*, outlined how the world in a state of disarray was the antithesis of the kind of world God intended humankind to live in. The ultimate revolution of Christianity was founded on the eschatological hope that the maladjustment of humankind will be corrected by the coming into glory of God's kingdom at the end of time in the establishment of a new human race where no fear abounds, only bonds of love. In the meantime, McCabe believed that Christians were to proclaim that they belong to this future by acting in the spirit by which the future kingdom is already alive in the present.[17] Clearly for McCabe, such scenes of human suffering as seen in times of war were intolerable to God and the kingdom of love proclaimed by God's son, Jesus, so they could have no divine origin or approval.

On the contrary, the characteristic solidarity of the Christian means that the world in which violence and destruction are wrought will hate the Christian for their opposition to the values that it espouses.[18] For McCabe, the Gospel of John, in its rejection of the world as it is, was very instructive for the Christian of today because of the growing awareness of the interlocking complexity of evil that grips humankind in the world. He believed that we have discovered a resilient and flexible system of human exploitation but have begun to realize that it is not, for the most part, due to the faults of a few wicked individuals. This system is sustained on a daily basis by millions of people just doing their everyday

---

17. McCabe, *God Still Matters*, 168.
18. McCabe, *God Still Matters*, 168.

thing, whether it involves being a parent or working as a teacher or salesman, for in doing so they are dominating, exploiting, humiliating, and tormenting people simply because this is the way their roles fit into the system.[19] Anyone who tries tinkering with the system and trying to change it from the inside only ends up being co-opted by it and working for it. The real "brotherhood of man" can only be talked of when this old system has completely collapsed and a radically new one begun.[20]

Rowan Williams, in his book *The Truce of God*, offered some pointers as to how prevailing attitudes have led us to such a point in human affairs that, despite all the current concern for individual "wellbeing," our corporate health as societies is being overrun by a pervasive sense of fear that has led to the kinds of conflicts that dominate the news and cause horrific suffering. Williams explained that the European/North Atlantic world, where Christians are the majority religion, is suffering collectively from all kinds of fears, from unregulated immigration and the loss of identity that goes with it to fear of a terrorist attack and the curbing of civil liberties that might arise from it.[21] These fears have arisen partly because the society has been either unable or unwilling to look critically at itself and change accordingly, hence the reluctance of its members to see themselves as anything other than innocent participants to the madness flowing before their very eyes. A case in point was the arms race after the Second World War between the Soviet Bloc and the West, which promised to bring both superiority and stability to the winner but rather resulted in a situation of mutually assured destruction. One side felt the other side was capable of inhuman slaughter on an unparalleled scale, so preparing weapons capable of an equally unparalleled scale of inhuman slaughter was felt justified.[22]

Williams threw a critical eye on the Christian church in the face of such a picture of a society infected by a pervading fear and

---

19. McCabe, *God Still Matters*, 169.
20. McCabe, *God Still Matters*, 170.
21. Williams, *Truce of God*, 10–11.
22. Williams, *Truce of God*, 12.

unwillingness to accept responsibility for its role in the interlocking complexity of evil that exists on the planet. He lamented that many times the church's interventions in the public arena on matters of peace, war, and international affairs were readily written off as being both abstract and amateur. This he believed was in no small part due to the fact that the inner life of the church is regularly the scene of bitter and destructive conflict, and so it would be in no position to comprehensively insist on the requirements that might address the corporate health of society.[23] The very existence of the church, however, at the very least represents the possibility of a global community aiming at unity in the face of a world that thrives on rivalry and containment. The church has a duty to query the myths of innocence that have sprung up around societies that aren't morally mature enough to recognize their complicit role in the interlocking complexity of evil that grips the world.

THE FALLACY OF A "JUST WAR"

An honest reflection is necessary on the harm that the existence of the just war theory has done in enabling countless millions of baptized Christians, in good conscience with God, to fight in wars throughout the centuries, which has led directly and indirectly to countless instances of terror and mass suffering. While the theory may have been intended to limit human societies' recourse to war, it has long outlived its credibility as a reducer of conflict in the world and has no basis whatsoever in Christ's teaching. It employs a logic of deceit completely at odds with the gospel and has led to a great deal of theologians on the one hand extolling the virtues of peace and then on the other finding it possible to rationalize the participation of Christians in wars that lead to massive devastation in terms of human life and the planet.

It is perhaps most starkly summed up in a stained glass window of the Basilica of the Sacred Heart on the campus of Notre Dame University in Indiana in the United States. Here the Virgin

---

23. Williams, *Truce of God*, 23.

Mary is illustrated with the baby Jesus presiding over the Battle of Lepanto of 1571, in which Christian and Muslim soldiers are engaged in mutual slaughter. The story goes that Pope Pius V sent out and blessed the Holy League Navy (the Catholic navy, which included the Papal Navy) to destroy the Muslim navy in the Gulf of Lepanto. Although apparently greatly outnumbered, the Catholics won the battle, which Pope Saint Pius V attributed to the rosary being prayed in Rome for a victory. Pope Saint Pius V declared October 7 to be the Feast of Our Lady of Victories because of her part in bringing a homicidal victory to the Catholic Holy League.[24] Churches named after Our Lady of Victories became popular around the Catholic world, including one on the Ballymun Road in Dublin. After Pope Saint Pius V's death, the next pope changed the name of the feast to Our Lady of the Rosary, which it remains to this day, and the battle itself has been viewed by some historians as a founding event for the shape of the modern world.[25] However, the change of name did not change the message from church leaders that this was a victory won with divine intervention and favor, giving credence to the idea that God, violence, and governance are firmly interconnected.

Fast-forward several centuries and an all Christian bomb crew, from the same country where the stained glass window resides, was blessed by their Catholic military chaplain and pastor, Father George Zabelka, on Tinian Island in the South Pacific before they unleashed the deadliest bombs ever dropped in warfare and killed over 200,000 men, women, and children in the Japanese cities of Hiroshima and Nagasaki in August 1945.[26] The use of nuclear weapons on Hiroshima and Nagasaki was justified widely by the winners of World War II as a means of ending the war quickly, and although these acts clearly violated the just war theory's prohibition on the deliberate killing of civilians, there was no question among the majority Christian population of the United States and beyond that God was anything but fine with the

24. Fields, *Lepanto*, 12–15.
25. MacCulloch, *History of Christianity*, 495–97.
26. Maguire, *Vision of Peace*, 87.

hard decisions that had to be taken.[27] Father Zabelka, on the other hand, after suffering a crisis of faith relating to the events he had been witness to, did an about-face on his attitude of justified violence and traveled on pilgrimage to Japan in 1984 to apologize to the atomic bomb survivors for his role in it.[28] His example of honest, prayerful reflection leading to repentance and a rebirth in the gospel of nonviolence is an example to the church today to renew itself to the nonviolent way of Jesus. Zabelka publicly repented, stating that the church had failed to teach gospel nonviolence: "I was brainwashed. You know, a whole nation was brainwashed. And the church, churches, accepted it."[29]

CHALLENGING THE MYTHS OF EMPIRE

It is part of the prophetic and liberating mission of the church to challenge the myths that maintain the status quo of imperial powers. Jesus challenged the myths of the empire and religious leaders of his time and ultimately suffered their wrath as a result. The story of the Gerasene demoniac (Mark 5:1–20), where Jesus confronts and liberates a man possessed with an evil spirit, is instructive here. Ched Myers offered a radically political and anti-imperial interpretation of the story, which is wholly relevant still to the broad Christian church in the times we are living in.

> Jesus' confrontation with the possessed man is a symbolic encounter between the sovereignty of God and the demon of Empire.[30]

The story is set in the gentile territory of the Decapolis, which Myers describes as a stronghold of imperial Roman culture and power. The name of the demon is "legion," the technical term for a Roman army unit and a direct reference to Roman military occupation. The possessed man, therefore, represents colonized

---

27. Maguire, *Vision of Peace*, 88–89.
28. Maguire, *Vision of Peace*, 89.
29. Zabelka, *Peace Is the Way*, 149.
30. Myers, *Binding the Strong Man*, 192.

Israel, tormented and fragmented by foreign domination; he lives among the tombs that represent social death and marginalization, a condition of people rendered nonhuman by systemic violence. Jesus liberates this man of the evil spirit when the demons are cast into the pigs and they drown, representing the subversion or judgment of oppressive economic-military structures. The story is full of military imagery, and the drowning of the pigs (enemy soldiers) as they charge into the lake is a clear reference to Pharaoh's army being swallowed up by the Red Sea in the climactic event of Israel's liberation from Egypt. The healed man becomes a witness or missionary to his own people, now freed from fear and domination and restored to a "right mind." The dehumanizing forces of empire have been confronted and dismantled.[31]

A key point of note for the church today, though, comes with the townspeople's demand for Jesus to leave their district after the exorcism, revealing their accommodation to imperial power and resistance to true liberation. They would have been worried about the consequences of such an "expulsion" of imperial power given their experience of the Roman scorched-earth campaigns of reconquest. It could be argued that given the alliance forged between the church and empire since the time of Constantine, the church today still suffers from the possession of the "demon" of empire, which neuters its courage to speak the truth of gospel nonviolence to the powers that be, lest it should suffer a loss of wealth, status, and power that it carefully built up over the centuries that followed this unholy arrangement.

A RENEWED IRISH CHURCH AS A LIGHT IN THE DARKNESS

Having experienced firsthand the brutality of imperial domination, the Irish Church is well placed historically to lead the nonviolent resurgence of the Catholic Church. It has the collective historical memory to speak to the world from the perspective of the poor

---

31. Myers, *Binding the Strong Man*, 194.

and oppressed, having lived through and survived a violent settler colonial past. It knows the cost of remaining true to the faith in times of persecution and it also has the distinct honor of keeping alive the Christian faith during the so-called "Dark Ages," a time when Ireland became known as the "land of saints and scholars." While a lot of people scoff at such a label, there is a large body of historical evidence to back up that claim. This is not to ignore that the church in Ireland has committed grievous crimes, especially in the recent past when it gained and abused its position as part of the ruling class in post-Treaty Ireland. Part of the church's nonviolent renewal should be seeking forgiveness for these horrendous abuses and trying as much as possible to make reparations for what was done. It must learn the lessons of its alliance with political power in Ireland and realize that its mission is distinct from propping up the kingdoms of the world.

The renewal of the Irish Church is dependent on going back to the roots of the Christian faith and following Pope Francis's directive to teach and live Jesus' way of nonviolent love of friends and enemies. To this end, there are inspirational figures in Ireland who espouse and try to live gospel nonviolence in their daily lives, and there are groups, communities, movements, and individuals dotted across the world that offer their witness and experience as to how this can be done.

GOSPEL NONVIOLENCE IN THE US AND INFLUENCE IN IRELAND

The US itself has a rich history of groups and individuals who have embodied, and dedicated their lives to, the witness of the truth of gospel nonviolence within the belly of the empire. When Pope Francis visited the US on one of his many missionary journeys, he referenced four significant Americans whose lives reflected values of justice, peace, and dialogue. Among them were three people who espoused gospel nonviolence as the central ethic as to how they were to live their lives in faithful witness to the nonviolent Jesus: Martin Luther King Jr., Dorothy Day, and Thomas Merton.

Of these three figures, Dorothy Day was probably the most outspoken critic of the institutional Catholic Church regarding its complicity in war, wealth, and political power. She had a deep love for the church and attended daily Mass, but her life was marked by a radical commitment to nonviolence and solidarity with the poor. Unlike most Catholics at the time, particularly the church's hierarchy, she opposed involvement in World War II as she believed that violence was incompatible with the gospel, as evidenced in the Sermon on the Mount, especially Jesus' call to love enemies, which was central to Christian ethics. She remained committed to gospel nonviolence during the Cold War arms race, the proliferation of nuclear weapons, and American military misadventures in places like Vietnam. The Catholic Worker Movement she founded along with French Catholic immigrant Peter Maurin at the height of the Great Depression in the US during the 1930s sought to be a radical witness to the demands of gospel nonviolence in service of the poor and in opposition to war and enmity. It led to the setting up of "houses of hospitality" to practice the works of mercy on the poorest in society and also to agrarian communities that focused on ecological sustainability and nonviolent resistance, living self-sufficiently off the land as a form of critique against industrial and military violence.[32]

Emerging out of the Catholic Worker witness to a new society in the shell of the old came theologically inspired acts of nonviolent resistance to the war-making policies of the US government. When the "Catonsville Nine," a group of Catholic activists including the Berrigan brother priests, walked into the Catonsville draft board office in Maryland in 1968, during the height of the Vietnam War, and burned around six hundred draft papers using homemade napalm, they did so in the spirit of the creative, active nonviolence taught by Jesus to his followers in the Sermon on the Mount. At the subsequent trial, Father Daniel Berrigan spoke prophetically about their action, saying, "Our apologies, good friends, for the fracture of good order, the burning of paper instead of children."[33]

---

32. Catholic Worker Movement, "Catholic Worker Farms."
33. Peters, *Catonsville Nine*, 120.

While most served prison sentences ranging from one to three years, Daniel Berrigan went into hiding for several months before being captured by the FBI.

Father Daniel along with his brother Father Philip Berrigan of the Josephite order later became central figures in the Plowshares Movement, a Christian nonviolent resistance initiative founded in 1980 that took its name from the biblical vision in Isa 2:4: "They shall beat their swords into plowshares, and their spears into pruning hooks." This was a more controversial extension of creative nonviolence, as it involved disarmament actions such as entering nuclear weapons facilities or military sites and hammering on nuclear warheads, missiles, or equipment and pouring blood on documents or war machines, while reading scripture or praying. Their actions inspired over one hundred similar acts of disarmament with the emphasis on nonviolence, faith, and prophetic witness, drawing heavily on Catholic social teaching and the example of Jesus. The price they paid for these discretions was lengthy jail terms, public outrage, and the rejection of their actions by some in church authority as lacking any theological basis.[34]

The influence of these actions of faith-inspired nonviolent resistance spread to Ireland in 2003 when five Catholic Workers entered Shannon Airport and hammered on a US Navy C40 transport aircraft, causing $2 million worth of damage, in protest of the Irish government's facilitation of US war planes flying through Ireland on their way to cause death and mayhem in Iraq. Their actions were consistent with the Irish bishop's statements of opposition to the war and the use of Shannon airport as a US military stopover. While there were no public statements that explicitly endorsed this Plowshares action, Irish Catholic leaders clearly framed Shannon Airport's military role as morally troubling and used biblical imagery of peace and justice that resonated with the activists.

There was a real sense of momentum behind the opposition to the Iraq war at that time, and this faith-motivated nonviolent direct action of resistance to the US military war machine could have been a moment for the Irish Church to push its weight behind

34. Laffin, "History of the Plowshares."

similar actions of creative nonviolence in the spirit of the gospel of peace. Daniel Berrigan visited Dublin in August 2002, and more than a thousand people turned up to hear from this prophet of gospel nonviolence. In 2006, a jury found the Plowshares participants not guilty of criminal damage on the basis that their actions consisted of a motivation to save the lives of the would-be victims of the US warplanes in Iraq. However, despite individual support from members of the church, this kind of faith-based resistance failed to spark a radical move on the part of the official church towards efforts to embody creative acts of gospel nonviolence. The Catholic Worker experiment in Dublin largely petered out over time despite the best efforts of veteran radical nonviolent peace activist Ciaron O'Reilly. What it showed in its short lifespan was that people of Christian faith, even with limited resources, could and should be part of the nonviolent resistance to war-making within the broader peace movement. At the very least, it sparked some debate within official church circles over what form opposition to war should take for followers of Jesus and whether destruction of property to be used for destroying human beings was within the realm of Jesus' teachings and example of active and creative nonviolence. In the end, however, the Iraq War went ahead and the massive loss of life, constituting what the church feared as a defeat for humanity, happened while the whole world looked helplessly on.

As the Iraq war drew to a messy conclusion, leaving a trail of destruction and instability in its wake, other wars took its place in the limelight. The development of a seeming permanent war economy prompted Pope Francis to call what was happening "a third world war fought piecemeal" that "seems 'permanent' and unstoppable."[35] That the pieces seem to be coming closer together in these current times with the outbreak of war in Iran, the dangers of a fully fledged third world war seem depressingly likely. On top of this, political instability is growing on the back of the refugee crisis caused by these conflicts and the climate catastrophe that continues to disrupt the lives of millions, widening the gap between rich and poor, while the prospect of a nuclear apocalypse

---

35. Francis, "Address of His Holiness."

is getting closer. The kingdom of God seems as far away as ever, and yet, in the midst of this growing global crisis, the Christian retains an eschatological hope in the ultimate fulfillment of God's promises at the end of time, a hope rooted in the resurrection of Jesus Christ, the coming of God's kingdom, and the renewal of all creation. In the meantime, the church is called to remain faithful to the teachings of Jesus and embody the kingdom, calling people to repentance and a new life in Christ. This new life in Christ has as its central tenet nonviolent love of friends and enemies.

THE URGENT NEED FOR LEADERSHIP TO TEACH AND LIVE GOSPEL NONVIOLENCE

The resurgence of gospel nonviolence under Pope Francis's leadership of the church has meant that it can become the cornerstone that informs the Christian response to a world in dire crisis. It will only inflame the hearts of the Christian faithful, though, if those in positions of influence and authority listen to the wisdom of those guided by the Holy Spirit, who have ears that can hear and eyes that can see, who can counsel the church to act in ways that are consistent with the nonviolent way of Christ.

The work involved in heeding Pope Francis's call to the church in his 2017 World Day of Peace message that "to be true followers of Jesus today also includes embracing his teaching about nonviolence"[36] is of immense proportions. However, the church has probably never been as well-placed to educate its members on the ways of gospel nonviolence given its global reach, vast resources, and the technological advancements of the times we live in. This is as true in Ireland as it is in any part of the Christian world.

One of the most important developments in the resurgence of gospel nonviolence was the creation of the previously referenced Catholic Nonviolence Initiative, launched by Catholic peace practitioners, theologians, and church leaders from around the world, including representatives from conflict zones. Following

---

36. Francis, "Nonviolence," §3.

the landmark Nonviolence and Just Peace Conference held in Rome in 2016, its purpose and goals included to mainstream nonviolence in Catholic teaching and encourage the church to shift from "just war" language to a framework of "just peace" rooted in active nonviolence and in promoting nonviolence as a spirituality, lifestyle, political method, and theological commitment. It sought to provide education and theological reflection on nonviolence for pastoral and global contexts, while calling on the church's magisterium to more clearly affirm Jesus' way of nonviolence as normative and central to discipleship. To support its work, it would develop resources and training in an attempt to embed nonviolence in parishes, schools, and communities.[37]

Pax Christi International was at the heart of this new initiative, and in response the Irish branch of Pax Christi cohosted a public event with the Trinity College Dublin Loyola Institute in 2023, where speakers Marie Dennis and Pat Gaffney from the Catholic Nonviolence Initiative presented on the urgent need and efforts already underway to integrate gospel nonviolence explicitly into the life of the church. Despite this, gospel nonviolence has yet to ignite the minds of the Catholic faithful in Ireland and remains on the margins of Christian consciousness still, despite the presence of many peace and justice groups in parishes dotted all around the island of Ireland. The absence of a papal encyclical on gospel nonviolence is an obvious barrier to convincing church leaders to use their resources on the promotion of active nonviolence as lived and taught by Jesus as a central ethic for which Christians should aim to faithfully follow Christ. Yet, Pope Francis along with theologians and the witness of those who have lived lives of active nonviolence have made it abundantly clear that this is what the church is commissioned to teach and live faithfully by. It is incumbent therefore that gospel nonviolence be taught to Christians, and the church in Ireland is well-placed to do this.

---

37. Catholic Nonviolence Initiative, "Our Work."

GOSPEL NONVIOLENCE AND CATHOLIC EDUCATION IN IRELAND

The vast majority of schools in Ireland are Catholic, and although there exists a desire on the part of many for more choice when it comes to their children's education, opinion polls have demonstrated time and again that most people are happy for Catholic schools to continue to play their role in Ireland's education system. What should set Catholic schools apart from non-Catholic schools, though, shouldn't just be the celebration of the sacraments or the prayers said at an assembly, but the enlightenment that comes from the knowledge and understanding of Jesus' revolutionary manifestation of the God of love and the implications that flow from that. Gospel nonviolence needs to be explicitly taught in both the primary and secondary curriculums. In the few textbooks where gospel nonviolence is referenced in the curriculum, it is usually portrayed as a tradition of a small number of Christians; no serious treatment or depth is given to the enormity of the implications for Christian living that flow from this. Children are the most vulnerable in society to the infestation of fear and enmity leading to justification of violent solutions to situations of conflict—from the subliminal messaging of children's cartoons to the vast proliferation of movies that promote the myth of redemptive violence. Schools are well-placed to counterbalance these falsehoods and promote nonviolent alternatives. The most obvious place to do so would be during lessons of religious education, but it could entail a wider cross-curricular approach, incorporating many aspects of the Christian message of nonviolence in subjects like history, politics and society, economics, and civic, social, and political education (CPSE), to name a few. The school calendar offers great scope to emphasize the Christian calling to live out nonviolence. Days of peace are already incorporated into the school schedule in most Catholic schools, but these can be truly invigorated with a focusing on the prophetic edge of gospel nonviolence and alternatives to the traditional reliance of most of the society on violent means when necessary. Of course, such education needs to be resourced, and the Catholic Nonviolence Initiative and the Rome-based Catholic Nonviolence Institute that arose from it need to ensure that the necessary resources and capital to finance them are readily available.

Such education on Christian nonviolence entails giving the educators that staff Catholic schools themselves the training they need to deliver this revolutionary content. For some, it will involve a whole new way of looking at the gospel and a whole new way of thinking. A superficial understanding of gospel nonviolence can also engender disbelief and resistance to the idea that Christians are to leave themselves more vulnerable than they already are in this world without the recourse to violent defense. As such, the process by which schools fully adopt the ethos of the nonviolent gospel is one that will require whatever time it takes for the Holy Spirit to work. It will require strong and courageous leadership, and so it is imperative that the leaders in Catholic schools are invited to attend conferences and events where gospel nonviolence can be unpacked and debated.

The university serves as a vital space for cultivating and disseminating knowledge of gospel nonviolence, fostering critical understanding and transformative practice. Currently in Irish universities there exists not a single course on the theology of Christian nonviolence, and it is referenced only marginally in other courses to do with peace and conflict studies. At the very least, they could offer undergraduate and postgraduate modules explicitly to do with the study of the theology of gospel nonviolence using resources from Pax Christi, the Catholic Nonviolence Initiative, and the extensive array of theologians who have made it their life's work to bring it to light.

None of this can be delivered by way of diktat, however. Belief in the saving power of Jesus and loving one another as he has loved is a choice grounded in the freedom of the informed human conscience. This conscience needs to be informed by a collective effort of all the different bodies that make up the church. As such it requires a lot of leadership from those most informed theologically on the truth of gospel nonviolence. That leadership exists in the Catholic Institute for Nonviolence, and they need the support

Gospel Nonviolence and the Renewal of the Irish Church

of the Vatican to ensure they fulfill their mandate to "make nonviolence research, resources, and lived experience more accessible to Catholic Church leaders, communities, and institutions in order to deepen Catholic understanding of and commitment to the practice of Gospel nonviolence."[38]

Church structures too need to reflect the nonviolent teachings of Jesus. The promised changes arising out of the synodal process already underway should see progress in this respect as regards the role of women and laity in the life of the church. There is still strong opposition to the idea of ordination to the priesthood being open to women and married couples, despite the strong scriptural evidence that the early church contained both these elements. A church renewed by gospel nonviolence would be one where positions of responsibility were decided on a more democratic basis than has historically been the case, leading to a break from the old tendencies of some to maintain an elitist hierarchy, far removed from the realities and struggles of people in everyday life. A clear motivation to serve rather than be served should lie at the heart of anyone seeking to enrich the ministry of the church, and it only makes sense that, after being excluded for so long, women and the laity in general be afforded the opportunity to enrich the life of the church and be part of a renewal of faithful service to the nonviolent kingdom of God.

---

38. Catholic Institute for Nonviolence, "About the Catholic Institute.

6

A New Heaven and a New Earth

G. K. Chesterton once remarked that "the Christian ideal has not been tried and found wanting," but rather, it has been found difficult and hence not been tried.[1] Nowhere is this truer than when it comes to embracing Jesus' teachings on nonviolence. Surrendering oneself to a level of vulnerability that does not allow the use of violence even for self-defense purposes is an utterly counter intuitive position for anyone to assume in a world fraught with so much evil and suffering. The mystery of life into which we are all born doesn't get any more comprehensible by living out a nonviolent existence and potentially shortening one's already short lifespan. Yet, this is precisely what Christians are called to do by their Lord and Savior. Saint Paul wrote in one of his letters to the Corinthians that preaching a crucified Christ was "foolishness to the Greeks" (1 Cor 1:23), the intellectual powerhouses of the known world at that time. It defied any standard of worldly logic that a man helplessly and brutally executed would exhibit any of the power and glory of God. The resurrection of Jesus from the dead changed all that, and human history has not been the same since.

---

1. Chesterton, *What's Wrong*, 99.

A New Heaven and a New Earth

For Christians, the wisdom of God is found in the Jesus story: his preaching and life given over to practicing nonviolent love of friends and enemies, culminating in the greatest intervention of God in human history by raising to life again his Son who had been rejected and murdered by an alliance of the worldly powers of his time. It is the resurrection that validates Jesus' teachings and example of nonviolence as the basis for Christian living. Survival in this world is no longer the number one value that human beings should aspire to; rather, Christlike love is all that matters. Living according to the teachings of Jesus requires a complete reordering of one's heart and mind. It is as much a scandal to the intellectuals of today as it was back in the time that Saint Paul was writing to give oneself over to obeying the commands that Jesus taught his followers to live by. It remains at once a stumbling block to nonbelievers and madness of the highest degree to live a life in faithful observance to the demands of gospel nonviolence in a world where more people than ever are dying in conflict given the proficiency of modern weaponry.

The logic of the world today still dictates that violence is necessary at times to protect human life on this planet. The problem with this is that wars are always justified by their perpetrators as being in defense of some higher ideal, usually the survival of the nation. This logic has for centuries corrupted the Christian soul to the point where the greatest purveyors of violence in human history have belonged to the Christian religion. This flies in the face of the God revealed by Jesus, a God of unconditional love in which no violence is to be found. Christians are called at baptism to join in on the revolution of love that Jesus started, assured of the promise of eternal life. Evil and death have no more power over faithful Christians because the death and resurrection of Jesus have destroyed them once and for all. Christians are free therefore to build up the nonviolent kingdom of God as inaugurated by Jesus without any fear of death. Jesus has shown the way, and he has commissioned his followers who make up the church to follow his example.

Christianity's Missing Peace
The Urgency of Gospel Nonviolence

We are at a point in human history where gospel nonviolence is more relevant than ever. It is the job of all members of the church, but especially those in leadership positions, to teach and live the commandment of love as Jesus taught and lived two thousand years ago. While this has been far from the case over the centuries until now, Christianity has been responsible, thanks to the workings of the Holy Spirit, of quietly transforming the face of the earth. We can trace the evolution of the most celebrated values of humanity back to the teachings and life of Jesus. Things like human rights, looking after the sick, including people from the margins, efforts to end poverty, among many others, can all trace their origins back the Gospels and the Judeo-Christian tradition. While the Christian church in a broad sense has been guilty of many horrendous crimes, it has also been to the fore in efforts to care for and nurture people, especially the most vulnerable and marginalized. It is now at a point in time where it represents the best hope for humanity to avoid its own annihilation. By trusting fully in the ways of God, it can finally bring to the world the full effects of the authentic Christian revolution of love and help save humanity from itself.

The Catholic Church, now under the leadership of Pope Leo XIV, still has a long way to go to be the catalyst for change. Despite the progress made in returning gospel nonviolence to the centerpiece of the Christian revolution since Vatican II, culminating in the papacy of Pope Francis, many challenges still remain. Pope Leo XIV seems to be following in the footsteps of Francis with his public statements condemning the horrendous suffering of war and calling for nonviolent peacemaking to take its place. Yet the Vatican is still protected by the army of the Swiss guards, and while they may look like quaint figures from a bygone era, they retain the use of the most modern weaponry to foil any potential threats to Vatican City. Faithfulness to the teachings of Jesus on nonviolence would entail this arrangement to come to an end, as naïve as that may sound to those who place their trust in realpolitik. What an example it would be to the world if the Vatican got rid of its army.

A New Heaven and a New Earth

LET US BUILD THE CITY OF GOD

In Saint Augustine's classic work *The City of God*, he attempted to write a complete Christian interpretation of history from the beginning of creation, where he saw two contrasting cities emerge side by side, that of the "city of God" and "the earthly city."[2] He was writing at a time when the end of human existence was thought likely, especially as the perceived eternal city of Rome fell into the hands of the barbarians. He sought to sketch out, therefore, not a theory of politics in the usual sense, but what the ideal of collective human life would appear to be in light of what looked likely to be its final moments.

The City of God was not an attempt, therefore, to draft a vision of what might be appropriate forms of associations between the church and its enemies belonging to the earthly city.[3] Rather it took a much more encompassing view of human history and examined how the hearts of people are torn between two loves, described in terms of cities that coexist until the end of time when the final judgment will see the citizens of the two cities separated and left to their distinct destinies.[4] Both cities sought peace, but it was only in the city of God that true peace could reside, as the only true justice that leads to peace was found here. The earthly city sought peace through the exercise of violence and fear, while it was through righteousness and adherence to God that the city of God achieved its peace.[5]

There is no doubt that the hearts of the church faithful are still torn between the two cities that have not yet seen their final destinies. The church has had a long history of alliances with powerful states and armies in the interest of "peace." A church renewed with the gospel of nonviolence has a chance like no other in history to break with the myth of redemptive violence and promote true peace that comes from the God of unconditional love.

2. Augustine, *City of God*, 11.1 (345).
3. Williams, *On Augustine*, 111.
4. Augustine, *City of God*, 15.1 (478).
5. Bretherton, *Christianity and Contemporary Politics*, 83.

Ireland has taken on leadership roles historically in the global church and it too has a chance like no other before in its history to renew itself with a commitment to gospel nonviolence. While church authorities in Ireland have a long way to go in restoring gospel nonviolence to the heart of the Christian mission, Irish society lends itself already to a vision of what a peaceful coexistence can look like in the world.

Despite the recent upsurge in intolerance to increased levels of immigration that has resulted in some unsavory instances of racist-fueled violence, Ireland remains a country of welcome and inclusion. There are a deep-rooted empathy and solidarity among many people in Irish society for the poor and the downtrodden, given the collective memory of colonial oppression over the centuries. The resistance to oppression has at times taken on a violent character, but there have also been many examples of nonviolent resistance in Irish history, including the invention of the word "boycott," coming from the refusal of ordinary people to pay exorbitant rents to absentee landlords in the 1800s.

There still exists a great sense of community life in Ireland, which is not always evident in parts of the world where a cruder form of capitalism has taken hold. Community life has been sustained by many groups of people but in particular by the presence of the Gaelic Athletic Association (GAA) in every parish in Ireland. Sports in general terms are a release valve for all the stresses of life and as such take on a massive role in maintaining healthy communities. The sporting arena has replaced the killing arenas of centuries gone by where people gathered to unite at the sight of human sacrifices. This, according to René Girard, temporarily strengthened the bonds of the community by satisfying their collective lust for the spilling of blood built up by the conflicts engendered by mimetic desires. Sports, although not all, are a nonviolent alternative to the phenomenon of the scapegoating mechanism that gave rise to human sacrifice. The GAA, as a sporting body, is unique in the sense that it bonds together people who live in the same communities and strengthens a shared sense of belonging. It is part of the fabric of nonviolence that already exists in Ireland.

The network of parish churches in Ireland means that the revolution of gospel nonviolence can spread easily across the island in a short space of time. Although there is a shortage of priests, there exists some optimism that the ministries of the church will be opened up to women and lay people, whatever their marital status, as part of the synodal process already underway. As it stands, though, the infrastructure for spreading the teachings of Jesus on nonviolence is already in place to ensure that the renewal of the Irish Church inspired by a return to gospel nonviolence is not some utopian ideal.

What this means for the future standing of the church within Irish society is unclear, but a strong prophetic voice for active nonviolence in response to the violence woven into almost every vein of human existence is surely one that will garner respect from people of all faiths and none. Pope Francis is proof of this, and the Irish Church should build on the job that he did to make the church a relevant and important voice in the world again. It will not be without its problems or difficulties, but Jesus never envisioned the world easily coming around to a revolution based on love. It is time for brave and prophetic leadership to give hope to a very troubled humanity. Let gospel nonviolence renew the global church, and let the Irish Church be a beacon along the road to the nonviolent kingdom of God coming on earth as it is in heaven.

Bibliography

Antonello, Pierpaolo, and Paul Gifford, eds. *Can We Survive Our Origins? Readings in René Girard's Theory of Violence and the Sacred*. East Lansing: Michigan State University Press, 2015.
Augustine. *The City of God*. Translated by Marcus Dods. New York: Random House, 2000.
Aulen, Gustaf. *Christus Victor: An Historical Study of the Three Main Types of the Idea of Atonement*. London: SPCK, 1931.
Bauckham, Richard. *The Bible in Politics: How to Read the Bible Politically*. London: SPCK, 2010.
Benedict XVI. "Address of His Holiness Benedict XVI: Meeting with the Members of the General Assembly of the United Nations Organization." New York, Apr. 18, 2008. https://www.vatican.va/content/benedict-xvi/en/speeches/2008/april/documents/hf_ben-xvi_spe_20080418_un-visit.html.
———. "Angelus." Saint Peter's Square, Feb. 18, 2007. https://www.vatican.va/content/benedict-xvi/en/angelus/2007/documents/hf_ben-xvi_ang_20070218.html.
———. "Angelus." Saint Peter's Square, Mar. 11, 2012. https://www.vatican.va/content/benedict-xvi/en/angelus/2012/documents/hf_ben-xvi_ang_20120311.html.
———. *Caritas in Veritate*. Encyclical letter. June 29, 2009. https://www.vatican.va/content/benedict-xvi/en/encyclicals/documents/hf_ben-xvi_enc_20090629_caritas-in-veritate.html.
Berger, Rose Marie. "Catholic Just Peace Practice." In Dennis, *Choosing Peace*, 167–200.
Boenig-Liptsin, Margo. "Responses to Jean Pierre Dupuy: The 'Intermediary' Case." In *Can We Survive Our Origins? Readings in René Girard's Theory of Violence and the Sacred*, edited by Pierpaolo Antonello and Paul Gifford, 267–73. East Lansing: Michigan State University Press, 2015.

Bibliography

Brennan, Joe. "Central Bank Commission Discussed Concerns over Its Role in Approving Israeli Bonds Documents." *Irish Times*, Mar. 31, 2025.

Bretherton, Luke. *Christianity and Contemporary Politics*. Sussex: Blackwater, 2010.

Burke-Kennedy, Eoin. "Despite the Politics, Ireland Is Israel's Second Biggest Export Market for Goods." *Irish Times*, June 8, 2025.

Butigan, Ken and John Dear. "Catholic Practice of Nonviolence." In Dennis, *Choosing Peace*, 125–45.

Cahill, Lisa Sowle. "Traditional Catholic Thought on Nonviolence." In Dennis, *Choosing Peace*, 105–24.

Catholic Institute for Nonviolence. "About the Catholic Institute for Nonviolence." Pax Christi International. https://paxchristi.net/the-catholic-institute-for-nonviolence/.

Catholic Nonviolence Initiative. "Our Work." Pax Christi International. https://paxchristi.net/our-work.

Catholic Worker Movement. "Catholic Worker Farms." Catholic Worker Movement (website). https://catholicworker.org/catholic-worker-farms/.

Cavanaugh, William T., Jeffrey W. Bailey, and Craig Hovey, eds. *An Eerdmans Reader in Contemporary Political Theology*. Grand Rapids: Eerdmans, 2012.

Chesterton, G. K. *What's Wrong with the World*. London: John Lane, 1910.

Crossan, Dominic. *God and Empire: Jesus Against Rome, Then and Now*. San Francisco: HarperOne, 2007.

Dennis, Marie, ed. *Choosing Peace: The Catholic Church Returns to Gospel Nonviolence*. Maryknoll, NY: Orbis, 2018.

De Roux, Francis. "The Church and the Just War Tradition." In Dennis, *Choosing Peace*, 167–200.

Farrell, Dermot. "My Heart Is with the People of Ukraine Whose Lives and Land Are Being Torn Apart." Irish Catholic Bishops' Conference (website), Feb. 26, 2022. https://www.catholicbishops.ie/2022/02/26/my-heart-is-with-the-people-of-ukraine-whose-lives-and-land-are-being-torn-apart-archbishop-farrell/.

Fields, Nic. *Lepanto 1571: The Madonna's Victory*. Oxford: Osprey, 2020.

Francis. "Address of His Holiness Pope Francis to the International Catholic Legislators Network." Clementine Hall, Aug. 24, 2024. https://www.vatican.va/content/francesco/en/speeches/2024/august/documents/20240824-legislatori.html.

———. "Address of the Holy Father: Meeting with the Members of the General Assembly of the United Nations Organization." New York, Sept. 25, 2015. https://www.vatican.va/content/francesco/en/speeches/2015/september/documents/papa-francesco_20150925_onu-visita.html.

———. *Against War: The Courage to Build Peace*. Maryknoll, NY: Orbis, 2022.

———. "Angelus." Saint Peter's Square, Aug. 18, 2013. https://www.vatican.va/content/francesco/en/angelus/2013/documents/papa-francesco_angelus_20130818.html.

Bibliography

———. "The Christian Life as Discipleship." Medellín, Colombia, Sept. 9, 2017. https://www.vatican.va/content/francesco/en/homilies/2017/documents/papa-francesco_20170909_omelia-viaggioapostolico-colombiamedellin.html.

———. *Laudato Si': On Care for Our Common Home*. Encyclical letter. Vatican Press, 2015. https://www.vatican.va/content/dam/francesco/pdf/encyclicals/documents/papa-francesco_20150524_enciclica-laudato-si_en.pdf.

———. "Nonviolence: A Style of Politics for Peace." World Day of Peace message. Jan. 1, 2017. https://www.vatican.va/content/francesco/en/messages/peace/documents/papa-francesco_20161208_messaggio-l-giornata-mondiale-pace-2017.html.

———. "Words of Holy Father Francis at Vigil of Prayer for Peace." Saint Peter's Square, Sept. 7, 2013. https://www.vatican.va/content/francesco/en/homilies/2013/documents/papa-francesco_20130907_veglia-pace.html.

Frear, George L., Jr. "René Girard on Mimesis, Scapegoats, and Ethics." *The Annual of the Society of Christian Ethics* 12 (1992) 115–33.

Fuller, Reginald C., ed. *A New Catholic Commentary on Holy Scripture*. London: St. Paul's, 1969.

Girard, René. *Battling to the End: Conversations with Benoît Chantre*. Translated by Marcel Baker. East Lansing: Michigan State University Press, 2010.

———. *I See Satan Fall Like Lightning*. Maryknoll, NY: Orbis, 2001.

———. *The Scapegoat*. Baltimore: Johns Hopkins University Press, 1989.

———. *Things Hidden Since the Foundation of the World*. London: Bloomsbury, 2016.

Hauerwas, Stanley. *A Community of Character: Toward a Constructive Christian Social Ethic*. Notre Dame: University of Notre Dame Press, 2005.

———. *In Good Company: The Church As Polis*. Notre Dame: University of Notre Dame Press, 1995.

———. *The Peaceable Kingdom: A Primer in Christian Ethics*. Notre Dame: University of Notre Dame Press, 1983.

———. "Repent. The Kingdom Is Near." In *Christianity and the Social Crisis in the 21st Century*, edited by Paul Rauschenbusch, 173–76. New York: HarperOne, 2007.

Hays, Richard. *The Moral Vision of the New Testament: A Contemporary Introduction to New Testament Ethics*. London: Continuum, 2004.

Hom, Mary Katherine. "Girard for the Uninitiated: An Introduction to Girardian Theory and Its Application to Biblical Interpretation." *Crux* 39 (2003) 2–12.

Horsley, Richard. "Ethics and Exegesis: 'Love your Enemies' and the Doctrine of Nonviolence." *Journal of the American Academy of Religion* 54.1 (1986) 3–32.

———. *Jesus and the Spiral of Violence: Popular Jewish Resistance in Roman Palestine*. San Francisco: Harper & Row, 1987.

Bibliography

Irish Catholic Bishops' Conference. "Irish Bishops Call for Prayer and Fasting for Gaza." Irish Catholic Bishops' Conference (website), May 26, 2025. https://www.catholicbishops.ie/2025/05/26/irish-bishops-call-for-prayer-and-fasting-for-gaza/.

———. "Let Us All Say: Enough . . . Stop the War!" Statement of the Spring 2024 General Meeting. Irish Catholic Bishops' Conference (website), Mar. 5, 2024. https://www.catholicbishops.ie/2024/03/05/let-us-all-say-enough-stop-the-war-irish-bishops/.

John Paul II. "Address of His Holiness Pope John Paul II to the Diplomatic Corps." Jan. 13, 2003. https://www.vatican.va/content/john-paul-ii/en/speeches/2003/january/documents/hf_jp-ii_spe_20030113_diplomatic-corps.html.

———. "Holy Mass in Drogheda: Homily of His Holiness John Paul II." Sept. 29, 1979. https://www.vatican.va/content/john-paul-ii/en/homilies/1979/documents/hf_jp-ii_hom_19790929_irlanda-dublino-drogheda.html.

———. "No Peace Without Justice, No Justice Without Forgiveness." World Day of Peace message. Jan. 1, 2002. https://www.vatican.va/content/john-paul-ii/en/messages/peace/documents/hf_jp-ii_mes_20011211_xxxv-world-day-for-peace.html.

———. "Peace on Earth to Those Whom God Loves!" World Day of Peace message. Jan. 1, 2000. https://www.vatican.va/content/john-paul-ii/en/messages/peace/documents/hf_jp-ii_mes_08121999_xxxiii-world-day-for-peace.html.

———. *Veritatis Splendor*. Encyclical letter. Aug. 6, 1993. https://www.vatican.va/content/john-paul-ii/en/encyclicals/documents/hf_jp-ii_enc_06081993_veritatis-splendor.html.

John XXIII. *Mater et Magistra*. Encyclical letter. May 15, 1961. https://www.vatican.va/content/john-xxiii/en/encyclicals/documents/hf_j-xxiii_enc_15051961_mater.html.

———. *Pacem in Terris*. Encyclical letter. Apr. 11, 1963. https://www.vatican.va/content/john-xxiii/en/encyclicals/documents/hf_j-xxiii_enc_11041963_pacem.html.

Jones, Parrish. "Nonviolence in Theological Perspective." *Church and Society* 96 (2005) 56–63.

Kirwan, Michael. *Discovering Girard*. New York: Cowley, 2005.

———. "Rene Girard and World Religions." In *Mimetic Theory and World Religions*, edited by Wolfgang Palaver and Richard Schenk, 195–214. East Lansing: Michigan State University Press, 2017.

Knott, Garland. "The God of Victims: René Girard and the Future of Religious Education." *Religious Education* 86 (1991) 399–412.

Laffin, Art. "A History of the Plowshares Movement: A Talk by Art Laffin, October 22, 2019." Kings Bay Plowshares 7 (website), updated Nov. 2, 2019. https://kingsbayplowshares7.org/plowshares-history/.

Leithart, Peter J. *Defending Constantine: The Twilight of an Empire and the Dawn of Christendom*. Downers Grove, IL: InterVarsity, 2010.

Bibliography

Levine, Baruch A. "René Girard on Job: The Question of the Scapegoat." *Semeia* 33 (1985) 125–33.
Lohfink, Gerard. *Jesus and Community: The Social Dimension of Christian Faith.* London: SPCK, 1985.
Lubov, Deborah Castellano. "Pope: Christian Reconciliation a Way Toward Peace amid 'Senseless' War." Vatican News, June 30, 2022. https://www.vaticannews.va/en/pope/news/2022-06/pope-francis-meets-with-ecumenical-patriarchate.html.
MacCulloch, Diarmuid. *A History of Christianity.* London: Penguin, 2009.
Mack, Burton L. "The Innocent Transgressor: Jesus in Early Christian Myth and History." *Semeia* 33 (1985) 135–65.
Maguire, Mairead Corrigan. *The Vision of Peace: Faith and Hope in Northern Ireland.* Eugene, OR: Wipf & Stock, 2010.
Marx, Karl. *A Contribution to the Critique of Hegel's Philosophy of Right.* Translated by Joseph O'Malley. Cambridge: Cambridge University Press, 1970.
McCabe, Herbert. *God Still Matters.* London: Continuum, 2005.
McDonald, Brian. "Violence and the Lamb Slain: An Interview with René Girard." In Cavanaugh, *Eerdmans Reader,* 345–53.
McKenzie, John L. *The Civilization of Christianity.* Chicago: Thomas More, 1986.
———. *The New Testament Without Illusion.* Eugene, OR: Wipf & Stock, 2009.
———. *The Power and the Wisdom: An Interpretation of the New Testament.* New York: Doubleday, 1965.
Merlo, Francesca. "Cardinal McElroy: Pax Christi's Nonviolence Institute Will Push to Peripheries." Vatican News, Sept. 23, 2024. https://www.vaticannews.va/en/church/news/2024-09/cardinal-mcelroy-pax-christi-nonviolence-institute-interview.html.
Musto, Ronald G. *The Catholic Peace Tradition.* Maryknoll, NY: Orbis, 1986.
Myers, Ched. *Binding the Strong Man.* Maryknoll, NY: Orbis, 1988.
———. "Confronting the Powers: Introduction." In Cavanaugh, *Eerdmans Reader,* 337–41.
———. *Who Will Roll Away the Stone?* Maryknoll, NY: Orbis, 1994.
Nicholls, Kenneth. *Gaelic and Gaelicised Ireland in the Middle Ages.* Dublin: Lilliput, 2003.
Niebuhr, Reinhold. "Must We Do Nothing?" In Cavanaugh, *Eerdmans Reader,* 259–64.
North, Robert. "Violence and the Bible: The Girard Connection." *The Catholic Biblical Quarterly* 47 (1985) 1–27.
Northcott, Michael. "Girard, Climate Change and Apocalypse." In *Can We Survive Our Origins? Readings in René Girard's Theory of Violence and the Sacred,* edited by Pierpaolo Antonello and Paul Gifford, 287–309. East Lansing: Michigan State University Press, 2015.
O'Donovan, Oliver. *The Desire of the Nations: Rediscovering the Roots of Political Theology.* Cambridge: Cambridge University Press, 1996.

Bibliography

Palaver, Wolfgang. *René Girard's Mimetic Theory*. East Lansing: Michigan State University Press, 2013.

Patrick. *Letter to the Soldiers of Coroticus*. In *The Writings of Saint Patrick, the Apostle of Ireland*, edited and translated by W. Stokes. Dublin: Dublin Institute for Advanced Studies, 1918.

Paul VI. "Address of the Holy Father Paul VI to the United Nations Organization." New York, Oct. 4, 1965. https://www.vatican.va/content/paul-vi/en/speeches/1965/documents/hf_p-vi_spe_19651004_united-nations.html.

———. *Populorum Progressio*. Encyclical letter. Mar. 26, 1967. https://www.vatican.va/content/paul-vi/en/encyclicals/documents/hf_p-vi_enc_26031967_populorum.html.

Pearse, Patrick. "The Coming Revolution." In *Political Writings and Speeches*, 89–99. Dublin: Phoenix Publishing, 1924.

Peters, Shawn Francis. *The Catonsville Nine: A Story of Faith and Resistance in the Vietnam Era*. New York: Oxford University Press, 2012.

Prime Time Team. "Dubliner Missing and Presumed Dead in Ukraine Had Spoken of Brutality of War." *RTÉ News*, Aug. 23, 2024. https://www.rte.ie/news/primetime/2024/0822/1466273-dubliner-missing-and-presumed-dead-in-ukraine-on-brutality-of-war/.

Rauschenbusch, Walter. *Revolutionary Christianity*. 1891. Published as *The Righteousness of the Kingdom*, edited by Max L. Stackhouse. Nashville: Abingdon, 1968.

———. *A Theology for the Social Gospel*. New York: Macmillan, 1917.

Rhoads, David M. Review of *Binding the Strong Man: A Political Reading of Mark's Story of Jesus*, by Ched Myers. *The Catholic Biblical Quarterly* 53 (1991) 336–37.

Rynne, Terence J. "Jesus and Nonviolence: Scriptural Evidence." In Dennis, *Choosing Peace*, 79–103.

———. "Responses to 'Nonviolence: A Style of Politics for Peace.'" In Dennis, *Choosing Peace*, 229–38.

Schlabach, Gerald W. "'Confessional' Nonviolence and the Unity of the Church: Can Christians Square the Circle?" *Journal of the Society of Christian Ethics* 34 (2014) 125–44.

———. "Responses to 'Nonviolence: A Style of Politics for Peace.'" In Dennis, *Choosing Peace*, 238–40.

Schwager, Raymund. "Christ's Death and the Prophetic Critique of Sacrifice." *Semeia* 33 (1985) 109–23.

———. *Must There Be Scapegoats? Violence and Redemption in the Bible*. New York: Crossroad, 2018.

Scott, Peter Manley. "Kingdom Come: Introduction." In Cavanaugh, *Eerdmans Reader*, 159–64.

Searle, Joshua T. "Is the Sermon on the Mount Too Unrealistic to Serve as a Resource for Christian Discipleship and Spiritual Formation?" *Journal of European Baptist Studies* 9 (2009) 38–50.

Bibliography

Second Vatican Council. *Gaudium et Spes: Pastoral Constitution on the Church in the Modern World.* Dec. 7, 1965. https://www.vatican.va/archive/hist_councils/ii_vatican_council/documents/vat-ii_const_19651207_gaudium-et-spes_en.html.

Stassen, Glen. "The Fourteen Triads of the Sermon on the Mount (Matthew 5:21—7:12)." *Journal of Biblical Literature* 122 (2003) 267–308.

———. *Just Peacemaking: Transforming Initiatives for Justice and Peace.* Louisville: John Knox, 1999.

———. "Just War and Nonviolence: Disjunction, Dialogue, or Complementarity?" In *The War of the Lamb: The Ethics of Nonviolence and Peacemaking*, edited by Glen Harold Stassen et al., 85–87. Grand Rapids: Brazos, 2009.

Taylor, Peter. "Behind the Mask: The IRA and Sinn Féin." Produced by Andrew Williams. Featuring Denis Faul. *Frontline.* Aired Oct. 21, 1997, on PBS. Transcript. https://www.pbs.org/wgbh/pages/frontline/shows/ira/etc/script.html.

Thielman, Frank. "The Atonement." In *Central Themes in Biblical Theology*, edited by Scott J. Hafemann and Paul R. House, 102–27. Grand Rapids: Baker Academic, 2007.

Thomson, John B. *The Ecclesiology of Stanley Hauerwas: A Christian Theology of Liberation.* Aldershot, UK: Ashgate, 2003.

Tolstoy, Leo. "Christianity and Patriotism." In *The Kingdom of God and Peace Essays*, translated by Aylmer Maude, 1–20. New Delhi: Rupa, 2001.

———. *The Kingdom of God Is Within You.* Translated by Constance Garnett. Lincoln: University of Nebraska Press, 1984.

Watkins, Devin. "Pope's April Prayer Intention: 'For a Nonviolent Culture.'" Vatican News, Mar. 30, 2023. https://www.vaticannews.va/en/pope/news/2023-23/pope-francis-april-prayer-intention-nonviolent-culture.html.

Weaver, J. Denny. *The Nonviolent God.* Grand Rapids: Eerdmans, 2013.

Williams, James G., ed. *The Girard Reader.* New York: Crossroad, 2000.

Williams, Rowan. *On Augustine.* London: Bloomsbury, 2016.

———. *The Truce of God.* Grand Rapids: Eerdmans, 2005.

Williams, Rowan, and George Weigel. "War and Statecraft: An Exchange." In Cavanaugh, *Eerdmans Reader*, 387–800.

Wink, Walter. *Engaging the Powers: Discernment and Resistance in a World of Domination.* Minneapolis: Fortress, 1992.

———, ed. *Peace Is the Way: Writings on Nonviolence from the Fellowship of Reconciliation.* Maryknoll, NY: Orbis, 2000.

———. *Powers That Be: Theology for a New Millennium.* New York: Doubleday, 1998.

Yoder, John Howard. "Just War and Nonviolence: Disjunction, Dialogue, or Complementarity?" In *The War of the Lamb: The Ethics of Nonviolence and Peacemaking*, edited by Glen Harold Stassen et al., 85–87. Grand Rapids: Brazos, 2009.

Bibliography

———. *The Politics of Jesus.* Grand Rapids: Eerdmans, 1994.

Zabelka, George. *Peace Is the Way: Writings on Nonviolence and Peacemaking.* Maryknoll, NY: Orbis, 1984.

www.ingramcontent.com/pod-product-compliance
Lightning Source LLC
Chambersburg PA
CBHW071622170426
43195CB00038B/2038